The Five Kingdoms

Name _____

Scientists have placed all living things into five kingdoms. The organisms in each group below represent one of the five kingdoms of living things.

Label each group using the words from the **WORD BANK**.

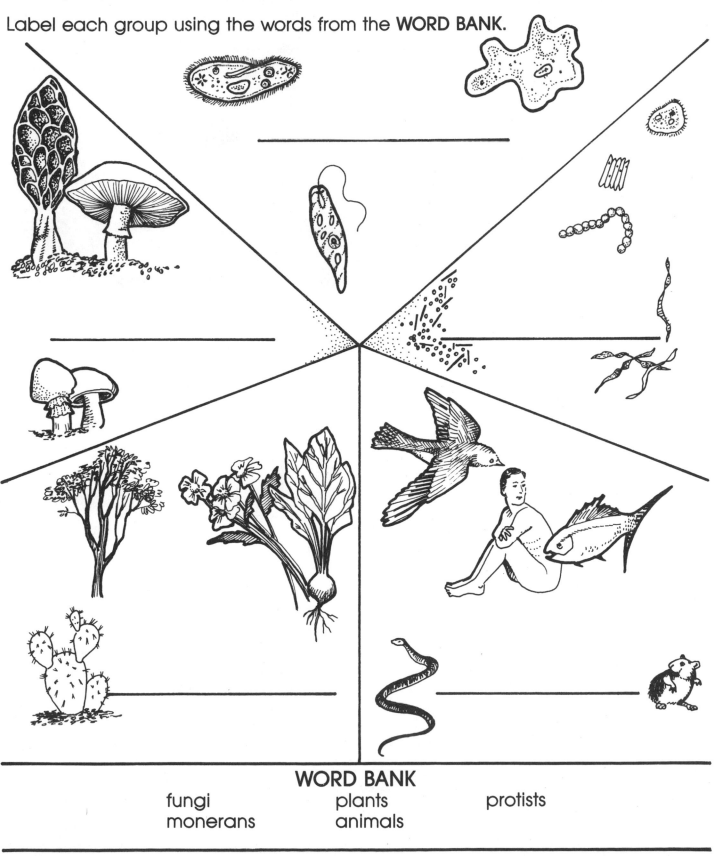

WORD BANK

fungi	plants	protists
monerans	animals	

Family of Living Things

Name _____

Scientists divide living things into five main groups called kingdoms. Complete the chart comparing the five kingdoms.

	Kingdoms				
	Animal	Plant	Fungus	Protist	Moneran
Does it make food? (Yes; No; Yes/No)					
Does it move about? (Yes; No; Some)					
How many cells does it have? (One; Many)					
Does the cell have a nucleus? (Yes; No)					

2

Animal or Plant?

Name _____

Most scientists divide all living things into five groups, called kingdoms. Two of the largest are the Animal Kingdom and the Plant Kingdom.

Compare these two kingdoms by using the chart below. Check the correct box or boxes next to each characteristic.

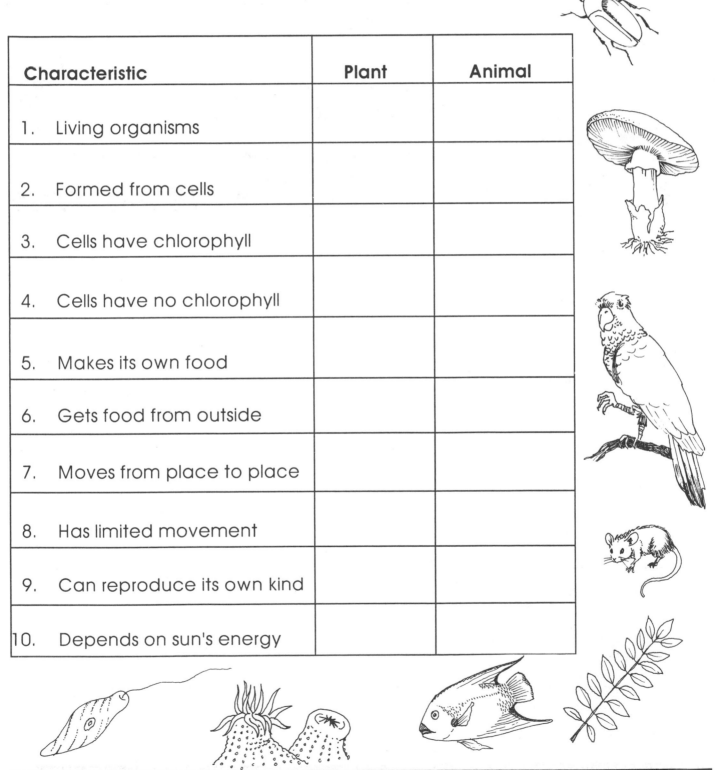

Characteristic	Plant	Animal
1. Living organisms		
2. Formed from cells		
3. Cells have chlorophyll		
4. Cells have no chlorophyll		
5. Makes its own food		
6. Gets food from outside		
7. Moves from place to place		
8. Has limited movement		
9. Can reproduce its own kind		
10. Depends on sun's energy		

The Plant World

Name _____

This chart shows how scientists group the many kinds of plants in the plant world.

Place a check in the column or columns that represent the plant with that characteristic.

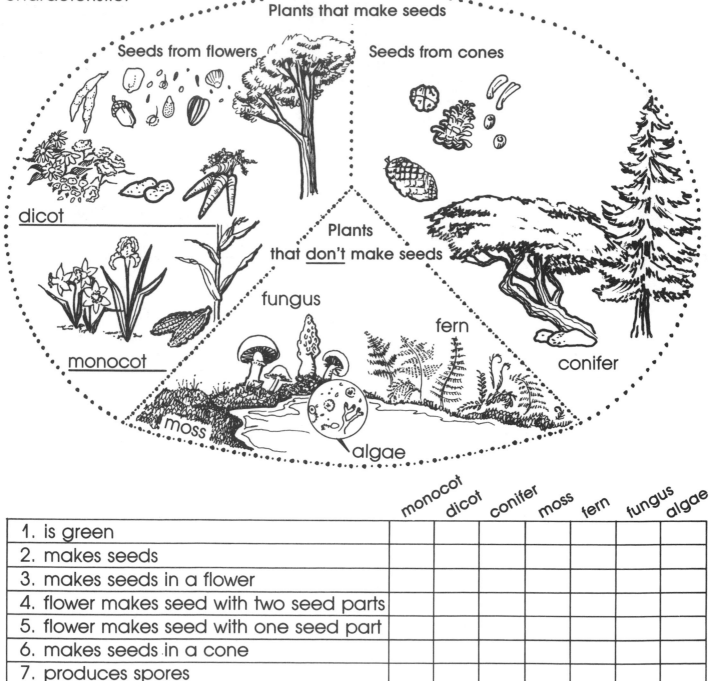

	monocot	dicot	conifer	moss	fern	fungus	algae
1. is green							
2. makes seeds							
3. makes seeds in a flower							
4. flower makes seed with two seed parts							
5. flower makes seed with one seed part							
6. makes seeds in a cone							
7. produces spores							
8. has leaves with veins							
9. has leaves with parallel veins							
10. has leaves with net-like veins							
11. has needle-like leaves							
12. one-celled plant							

Plant Parts

Label the parts of the bean plant using the words from the **WORD BANK**.

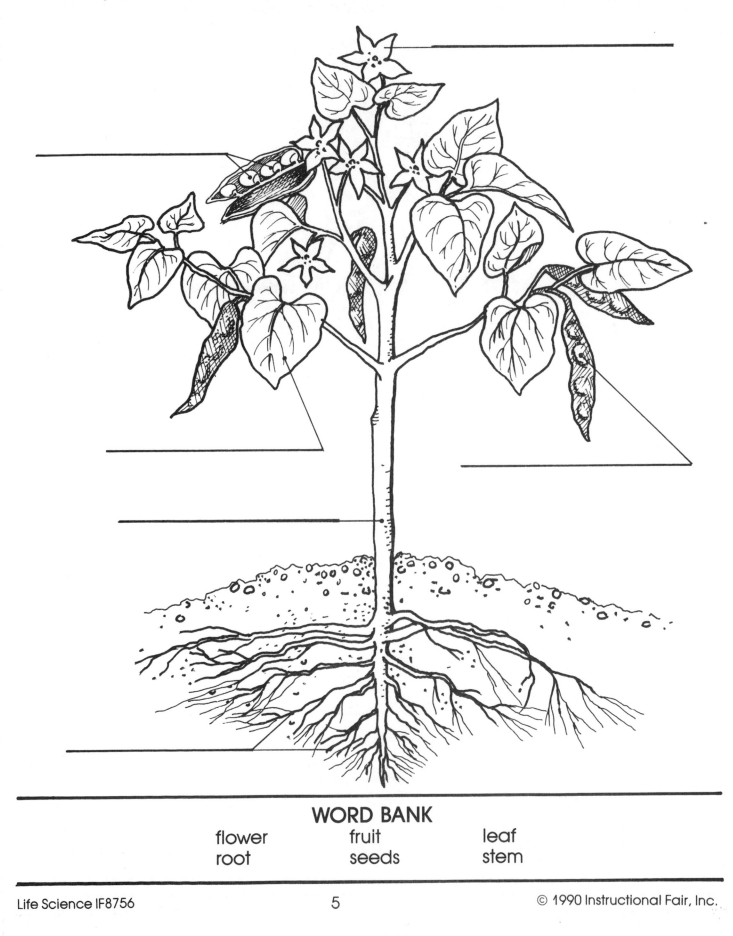

WORD BANK

flower	fruit	leaf
root	seeds	stem

5

A Flowering Plant

Name _____

Label the parts of this flowering plant.

WORD BANK

roots	stem	leaf
flower	petal	sepal
stamen	pistil	

Flower Parts

Use the words from the **WORD BANK** to label the parts of the two flowers below.

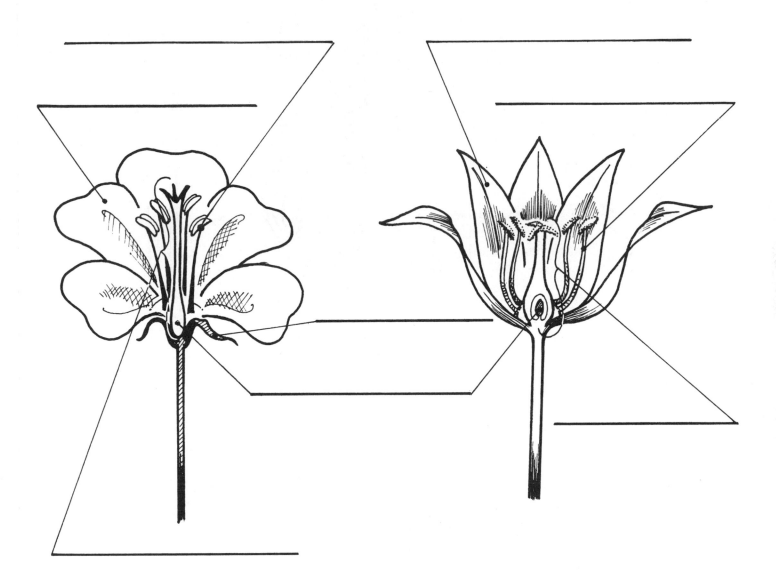

WORD BANK

ovary	petal	pistil
sepal	stamen	

Seed-Producing Parts of a Flower

Name _____

Label the seed-producing parts of the flower.

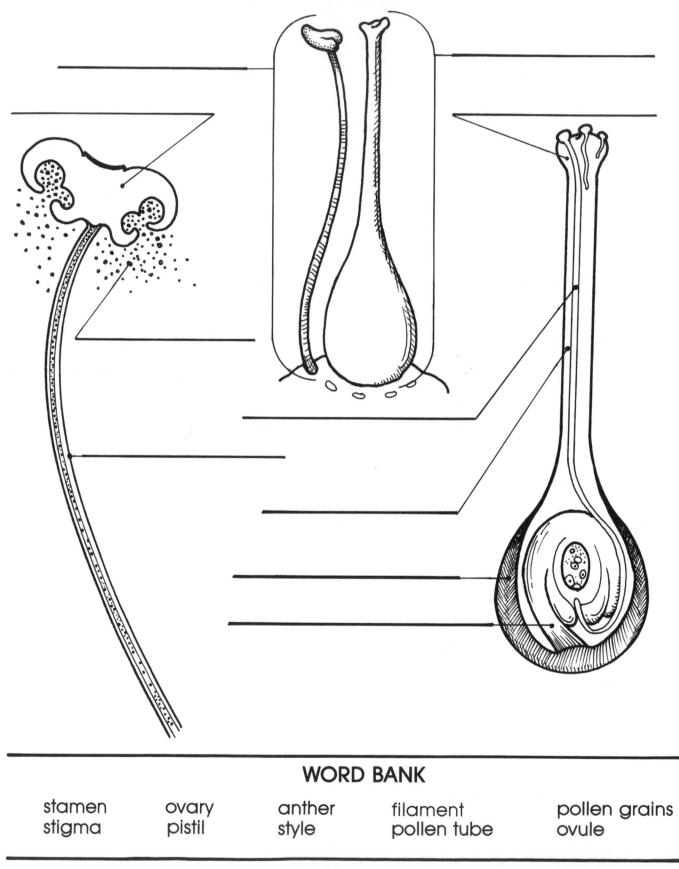

WORD BANK

stamen	ovary	anther	filament	pollen grains
stigma	pistil	style	pollen tube	ovule

Pollination

Label the main parts that are involved in pollination. Label the two kinds of pollination.

WORD BANK

cross-pollination	pollen grains	anther
self-pollination	ovary	pistil
stigma	style	stamen

Monocot or Dicot?

Look carefully at the plant parts and describe the characteristic that makes the plant either a dicot or a monocot. Then label the plant part either dicot or monocot.

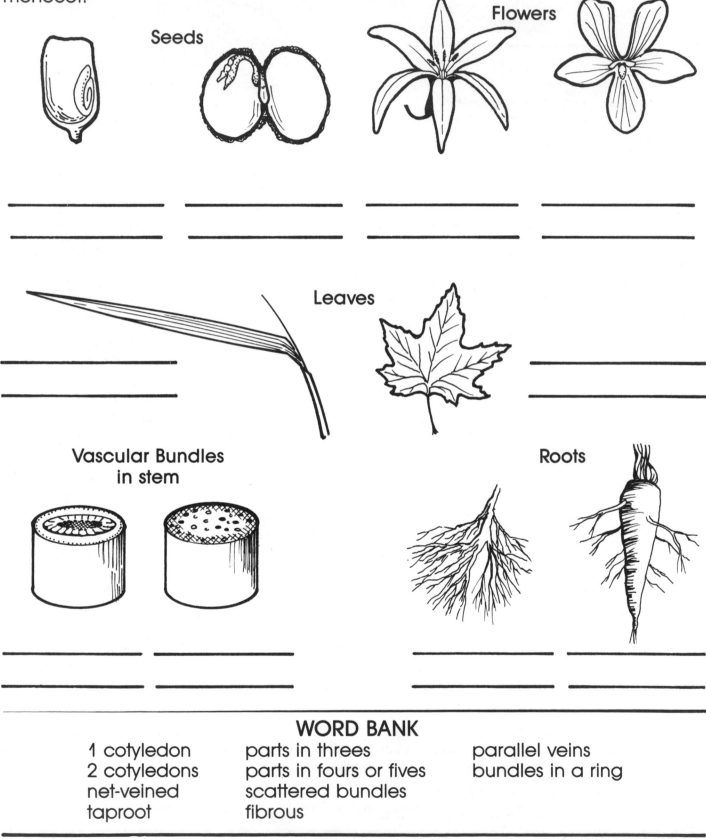

Seeds

Flowers

Leaves

Vascular Bundles in stem

Roots

WORD BANK

1 cotyledon	parts in threes	parallel veins
2 cotyledons	parts in fours or fives	bundles in a ring
net-veined	scattered bundles	
taproot	fibrous	

Eating Plant Parts

Label the parts of these plants that you eat.

_____   _____

_____   _____   _____

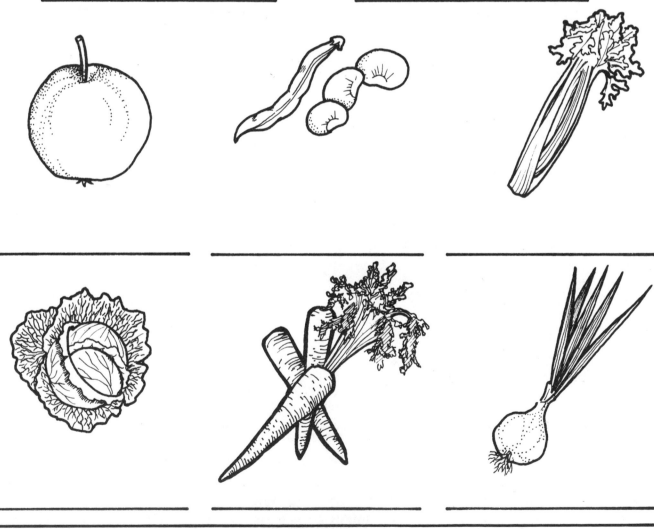

_____   _____   _____

WORD BANK

leaves	stem	seed	flower
fruit	bulb	tuber	root

11   © 1990 Instructional Fair, Inc.

Corn Grain

Label the parts of the corn grain.

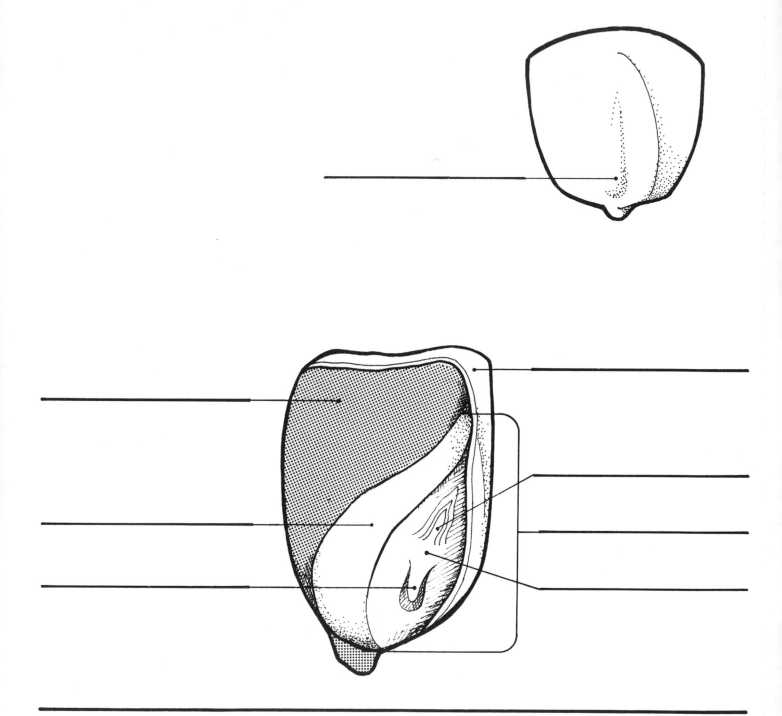

WORD BANK

cotyledon (food)   embryo   seed and fruit coats
endosperm   epicotyl (leaves)   hypocotyl (stem)
radicle (root)

     12

Bean Seed

Label the parts of the bean seed.

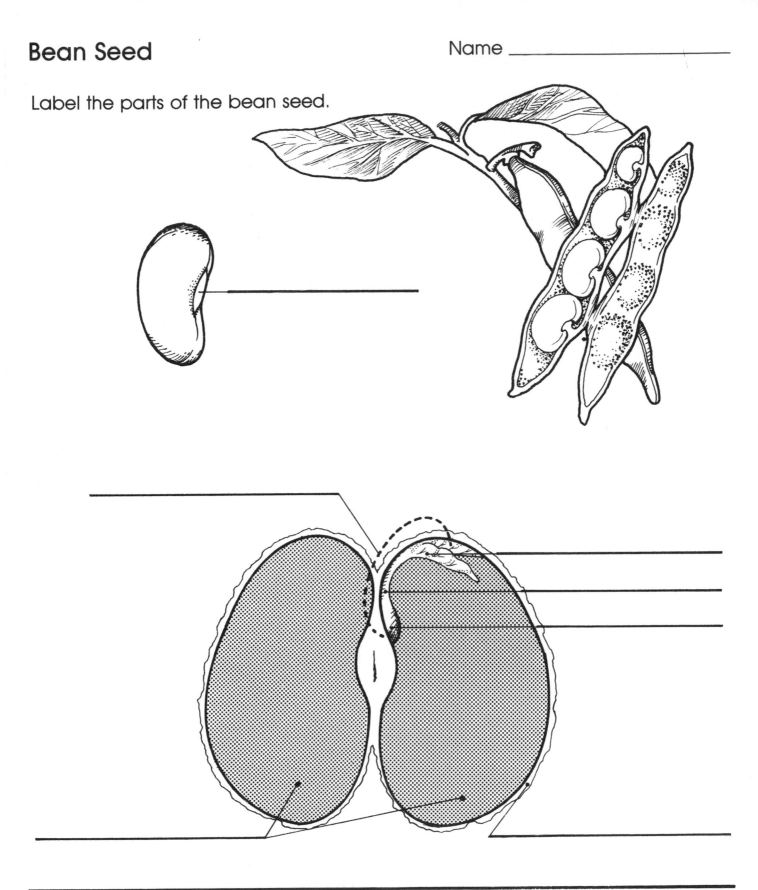

WORD BANK

cotyledon (food)	seed coat	embryo	hilum
epicotyl (leaves)	hypocotyl (stem)	radicle (root)	

Growing Bean Seeds

Name _____

Label the parts of the growing bean plant.

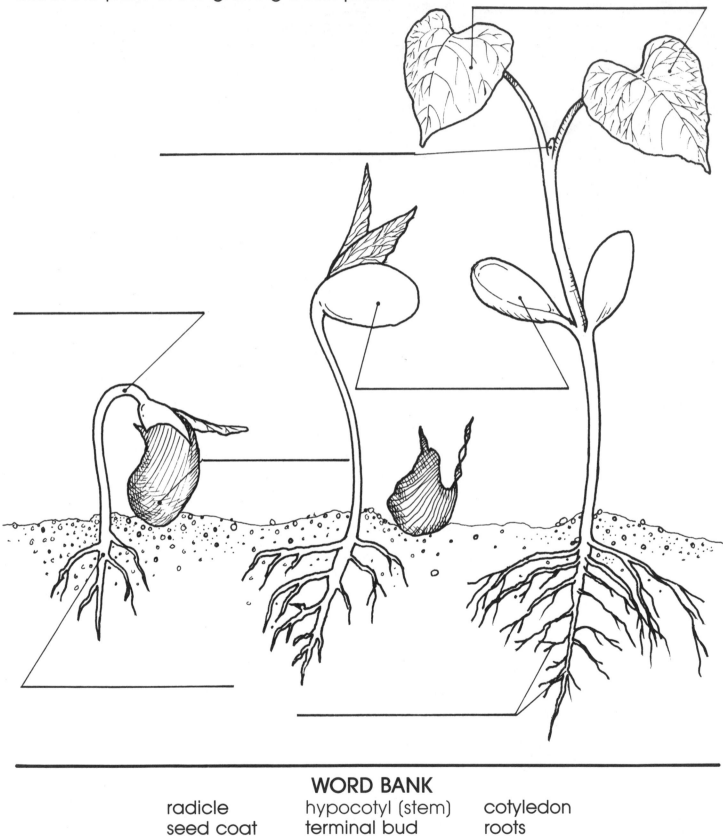

_____

WORD BANK

radicle   hypocotyl (stem)   cotyledon
seed coat   terminal bud   roots
first leaves

_____

Tropisms

Tropism occurs when a plant bends in response to outside stimuli such as light, gravity or water. Three common types are: **geotropism** which is caused by gravity; **phototropism** which is caused by light; and **hydrotropism** which is caused by water.

Label the type of tropism that is affecting the plant in each picture.

_____   _____   _____

Make a Prediction

The flowerpot in the first picture was placed on its side. The plant will continue to receive water and light. How will the plant's growth be affected after three weeks of lying on its side?

Draw a picture of what the plant will look like after three weeks.

Before   **Three Weeks Later**

Traveling Seeds

Name _____

Seeds are dispersed, or scattered, from the parent plant in many ways. The pictures below show six examples of how seeds can be dispersed.

Explain how the seeds are being dispersed in each picture.

1. _____

_____

2. _____

_____

3. _____

_____

4. _____

_____

5. _____

_____

6. _____

_____

Food Factories

Leaves are the "food factories" for green plants. Label the parts of the leaf below.

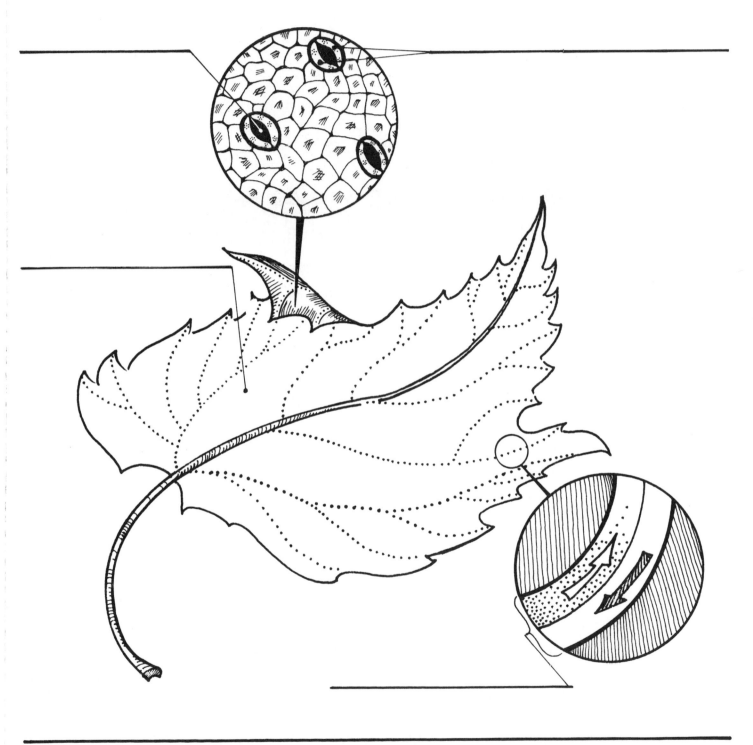

WORD BANK

guard cells   stomata
waxy layer   vein

Leaf Cross Section

Name _____

Label the parts from this cross section of a leaf.

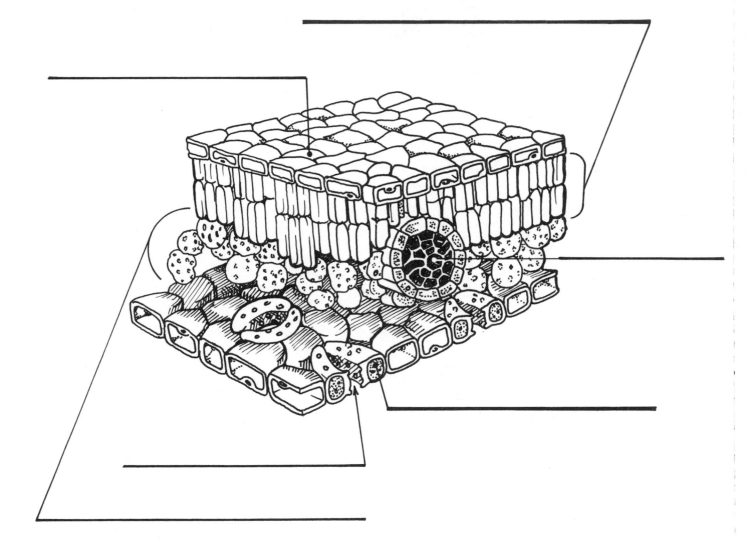

WORD BANK

epidermis	stoma	guard cell
vein	palisade layer	spongy layer

Let's Look at a Leaf!

Name _____

Before you can use leaves to help you identify plants, you must know the parts of a leaf. Label the parts of the leaves below.

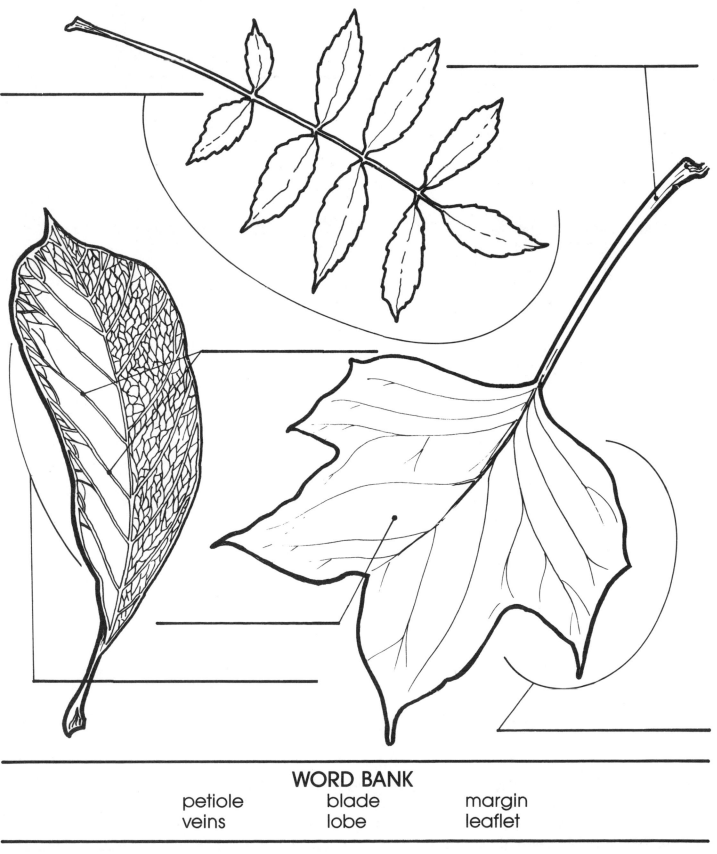

WORD BANK

petiole	blade	margin
veins	lobe	leaflet

Leaf Shapes

Name _____

Label the different characteristics of each group of leaves.

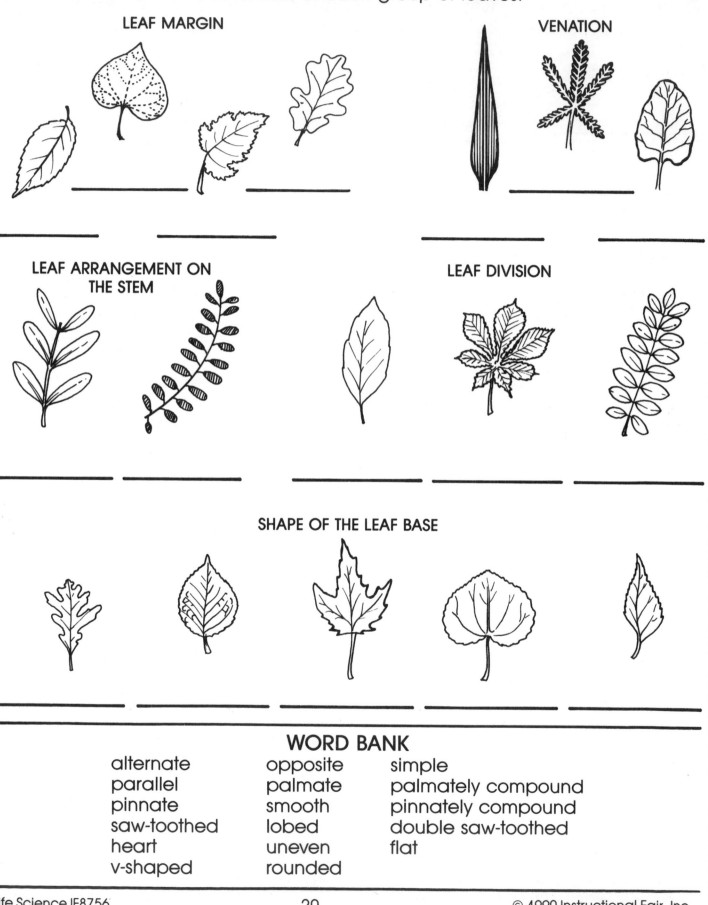

LEAF MARGIN

_____ _____

_____ _____

VENATION

_____ _____

**LEAF ARRANGEMENT ON
THE STEM**

_____ _____

LEAF DIVISION

_____ _____ _____

SHAPE OF THE LEAF BASE

_____ _____ _____ _____ _____

WORD BANK

alternate	opposite	simple
parallel	palmate	palmately compound
pinnate	smooth	pinnately compound
saw-toothed	lobed	double saw-toothed
heart	uneven	flat
v-shaped	rounded	

A Key to Trees

A scientist may use a key to identify a tree by its leaves.

Use the following key to identify the leaves pictured on this page.
The first one is done for you.

white pine _____

1. a. The tree has needles .... go to 2
   b. The tree has leaves .... go to 5
2. a. The needles are in bundles .... go to 3
   b. The needles are scale-like .... white cedar
3. a. There are 5 needles .... white pine
   b. There are 2 needles .... go to 4
4. a. The needles are thick and spread
      away from each other .... jack pine
   b. The needles are long and thin .... red pine
5. a. The leaves are simple .... go to 8
   b. The leaves are compound .... go to 6
6. a. The leaflets radiate from one point .... go to 7
   b. The leaflets do not radiate from one point .. white ash
7. a. There are 5 leaflets.. buckeye
   b. There are 7 leaflets............................... horse chestnut
8. a. The leaf has notches... go to 9
   b. The leaf does not have notches .... go to 10
9. a. The notches are pointed .... silver maple
   b. The notches are rounded .... sugar maple
10. a. The leaf is tapered at both ends .... dogwood
    b. The leaf is heart-shaped .... catalpa

The Tree

Name _____

Label the three main parts of a tree and the types of tissues in its trunk.

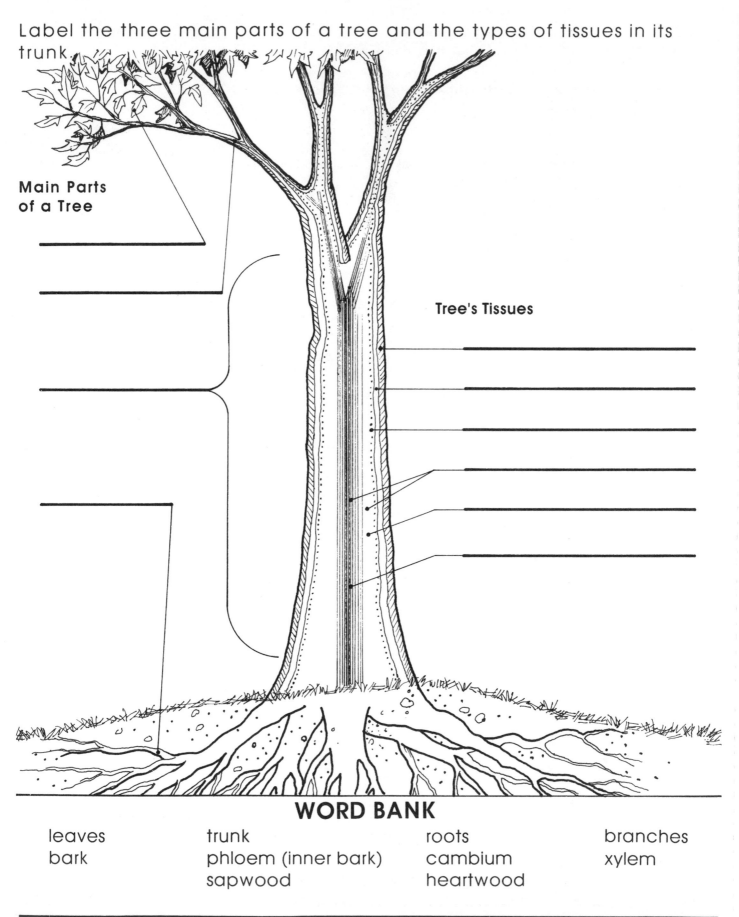

Main Parts of a Tree

Tree's Tissues

WORD BANK

leaves   trunk   roots   branches
bark   phloem (inner bark)   cambium   xylem
      sapwood   heartwood

Tree Stems

Label the parts of this tree stem.

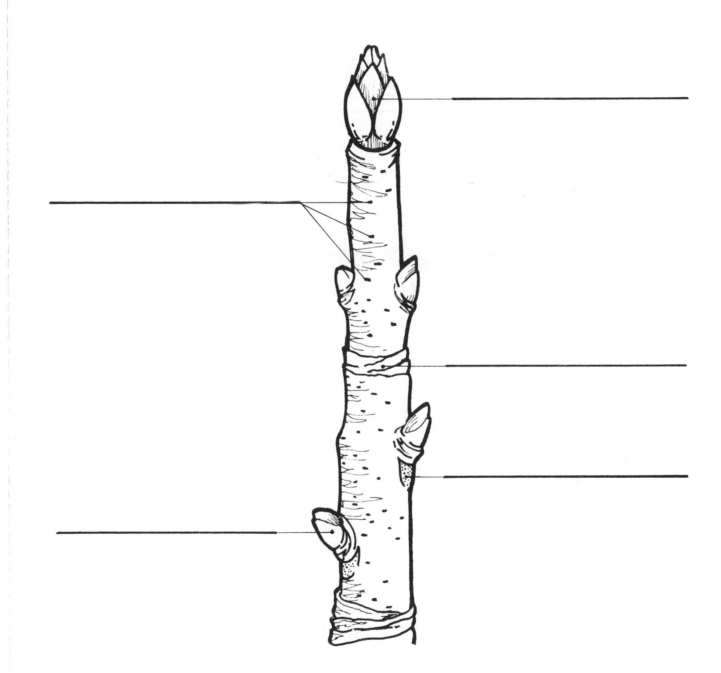

WORD BANK

end bud	side bud	leaf scar
air opening	bud-scale scar	

23

Inside a Tree Trunk

Label the parts of this cross section of a tree trunk.

Name _____

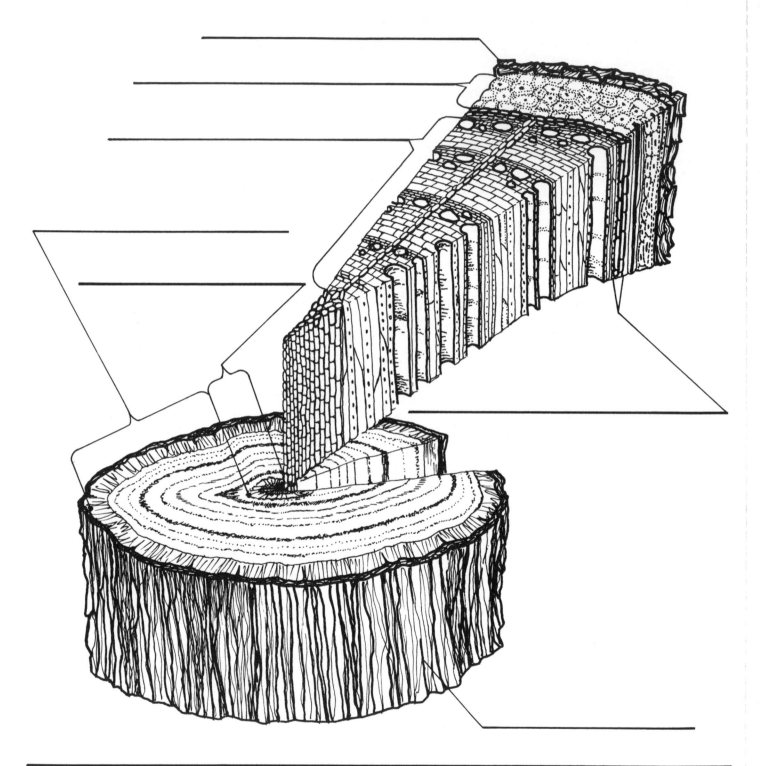

WORD BANK

heartwood   sapwood   bark
xylem   phloem   vascular cambium

Tree History

A freshly cut tree stump can be read like a history book. Label the parts of the tree, then study the annual rings, scars and cuts. Tell what you think happened to the tree.

Tree story:

_____

_____

_____

_____

_____

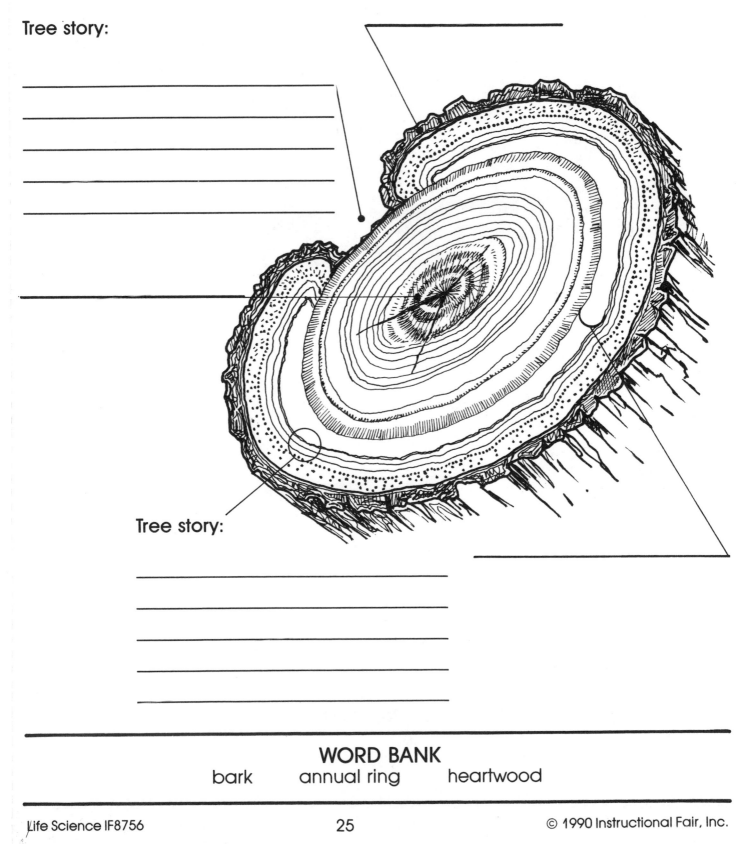

Tree story:

_____

_____

_____

_____

_____

WORD BANK
bark   annual ring   heartwood

25

Underground Stems

Tubers, rhizomes and bulbs are three types of underground stems. Label each of these types and their parts.

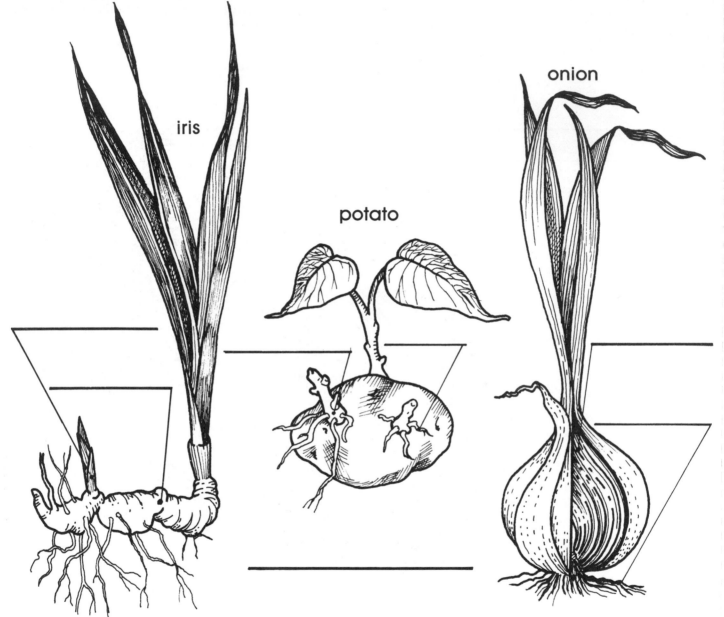

iris

potato

onion

WORD BANK

bud	leaf	root
stem	RHIZOME	TUBER
BULB		

Root Systems

Label the two root systems pictured below:

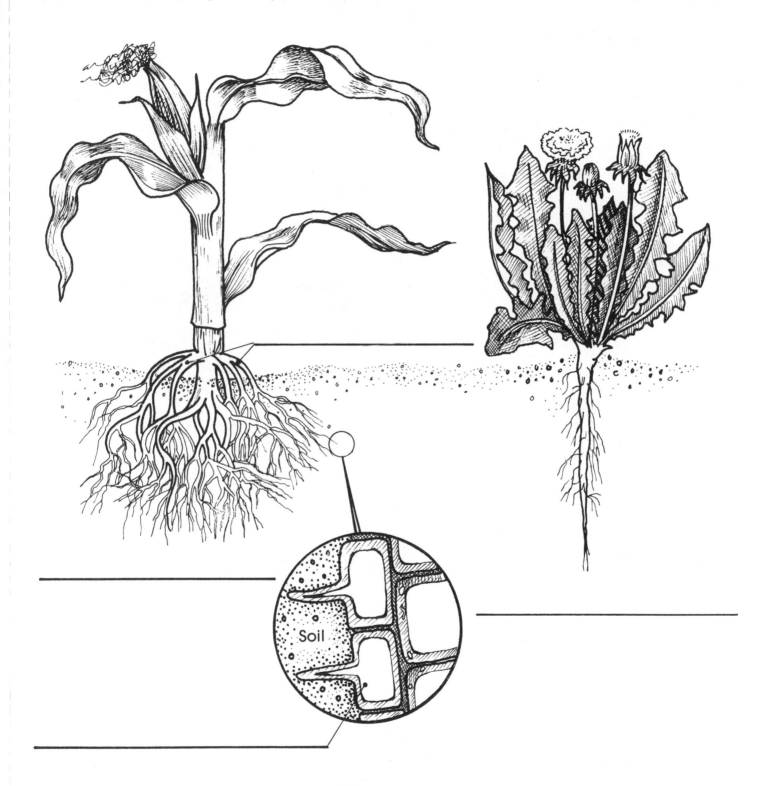

_____

_____

Soil

_____

WORD BANK

fibrous root system   root hair cell
taproot system   prop roots

Inside a Root

Below are two views of a root. Label both the top cross section and side cross section views.

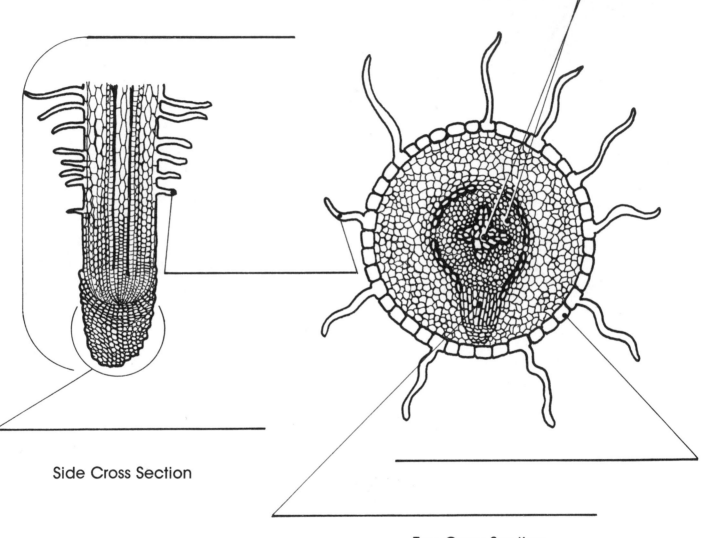

Side Cross Section

Top Cross Section
of a Young Root

WORD BANK

root hairs	root cap	root tip
surface layer	branch root	food and water carrying tissues

Life Cycle of a Conifer

Name _____

Label the active parts in the life cycle of a conifer tree.

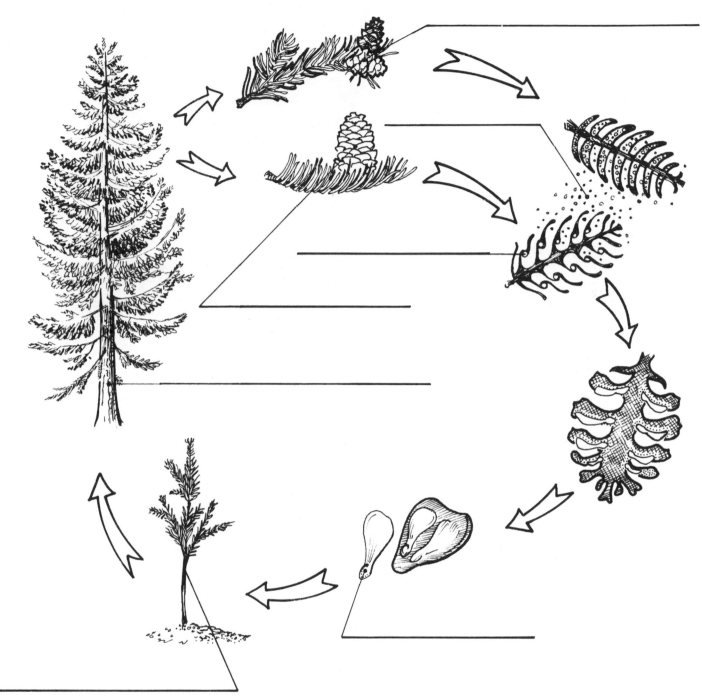

_____

WORD BANK

male cone	female cone	pollen
ovule	seed	seedling
mature conifer tree		

Ferns

Label the parts of the fern.

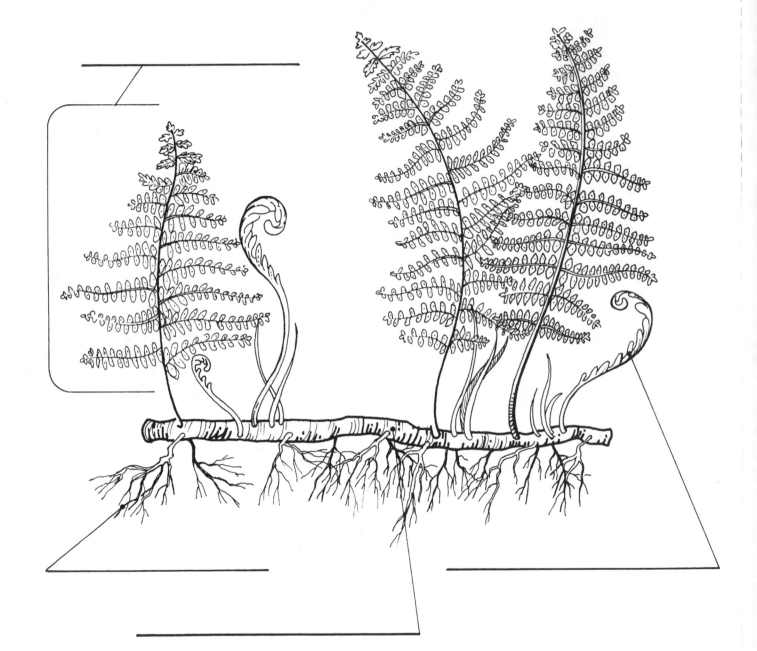

WORD BANK

frond   fiddlehead   rhizome
root

The Growth of a Mushroom

Name _____

Label the parts of the mushroom.

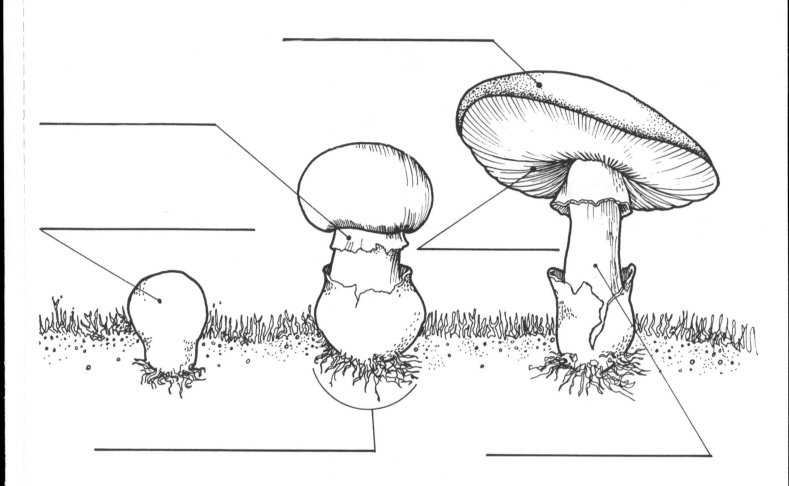

WORD BANK

cap	gills	stalk	filament
mycelium	membrane	veil	

31

Animal Kingdom

The animal kingdom is often divided into **subgroups called phyla.**

Draw a line from each phylum to the animal that belongs in it. Then draw a line from each animal to its characteristics.

PHYLUM	ANIMAL	CHARACTERISTICS

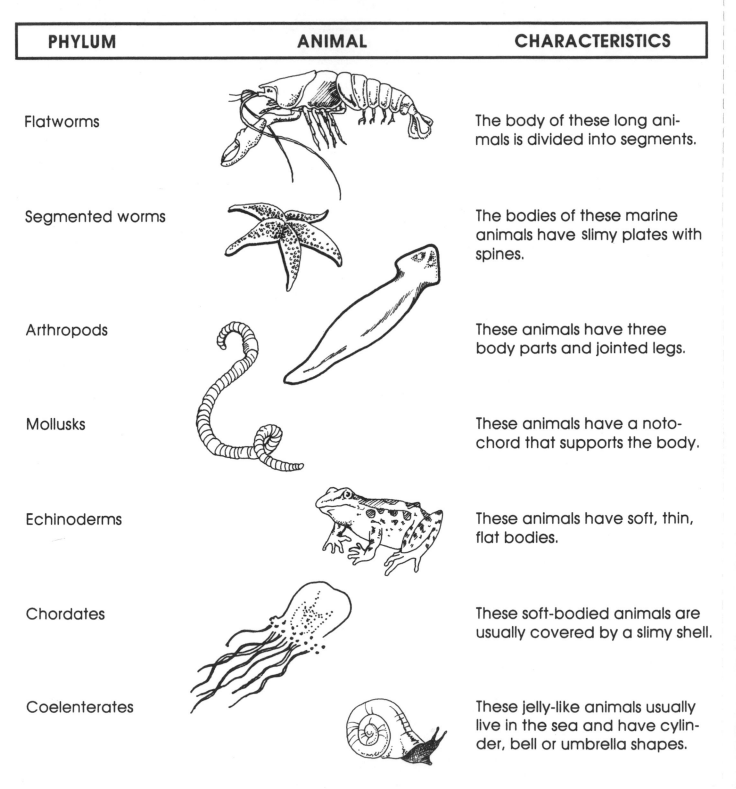

Flatworms

Segmented worms

Arthropods

Mollusks

Echinoderms

Chordates

Coelenterates

The body of these long animals is divided into segments.

The bodies of these marine animals have slimy plates with spines.

These animals have three body parts and jointed legs.

These animals have a notochord that supports the body.

These animals have soft, thin, flat bodies.

These soft-bodied animals are usually covered by a slimy shell.

These jelly-like animals usually live in the sea and have cylinder, bell or umbrella shapes.

Circulatory Systems

Name _____

The circulatory system carries material to every part of the body. It then picks up waste to be removed from the body. Circulatory systems function in their own special way.

Label the parts of the circulatory system for each animal pictured below.

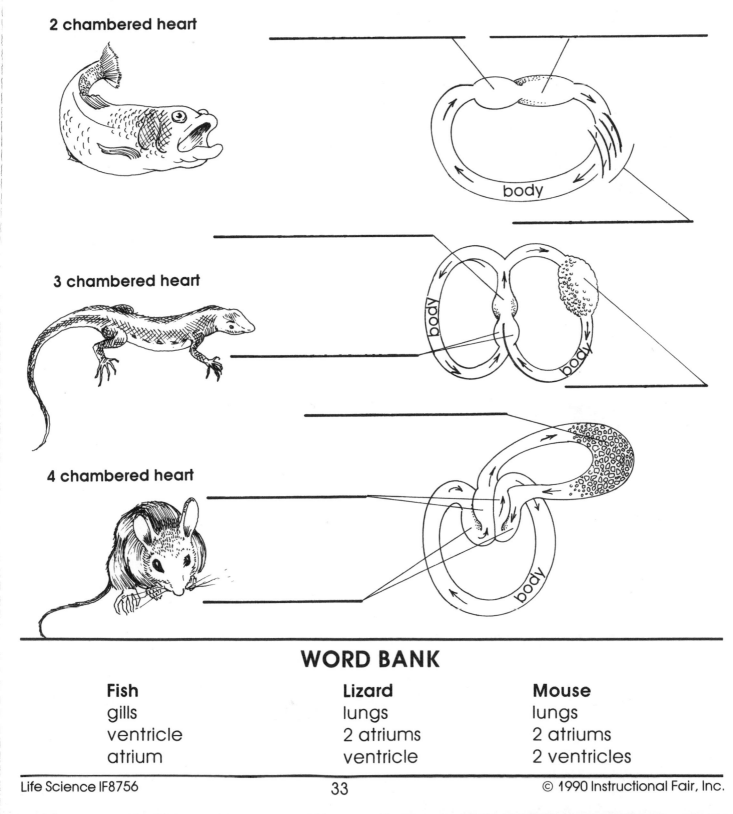

2 chambered heart

3 chambered heart

4 chambered heart

body

body

body

WORD BANK

Fish	**Lizard**	**Mouse**
gills	lungs	lungs
ventricle	2 atriums	2 atriums
atrium	ventricle	2 ventricles

Animal Defenses

Name _____

Each of the animals on this page has a special defensive adaptation.

a. Name the animal.

b. Describe its defensive adaptation.

a. _____
b. _____
_____

a. _____
b. _____
_____

a. _____
b. _____
_____

a. _____
b. _____
_____

a. _____
b. _____
_____

a. _____
b. _____
_____

WORD BANK

opossum	turtle	walking stick
ostrich	skunk	porcupine

Locomotion

Name _____

Animals have adaptations that allow them to move from place to place in a very special way.

Complete the chart by giving a one-word description of each animal's primary method of moving (locomotion).

Name the body parts involved in this movement.

	Method of Locomotion	Body Parts That Allow This Kind of Movement
rabbit		
fish		
mole		
blue bird		
spider monkey		
tree frog		

Symmetrical Critters

Name _____

There are three kinds of symmetry: radial, bilateral, and asymmetrical.

From the descriptions below, label the kind of symmetry each of these animals has.

Animal	Kind of Symmetry
snail	
starfish	
jellyfish	
angelfish	
sea anemone	
frog	
sponge	
spider	
butterfly	
lobster	

Types of Symmetry

radial: The body parts are symmetrical around a central point.

bilateral: The left and right sides are alike and equally proportional.

asymmetrical: These animals do not have a definite shape and therefore, no symmetry.

What's a Vertebrate?

Name _____

Vertebrates are grouped into five different classes. How are these classes alike, and how are they different? Complete the chart.

	fish	amphibian	bird	reptile	mammal
body covering					
warm or cold-blooded					
habitat					
born alive or hatched					
lungs or gills					
chambers in heart					

Classifying Vertebrates

Name _____

Vertebrates are sorted into five main groups called classes. Write the name of the class for each of these vertebrates.

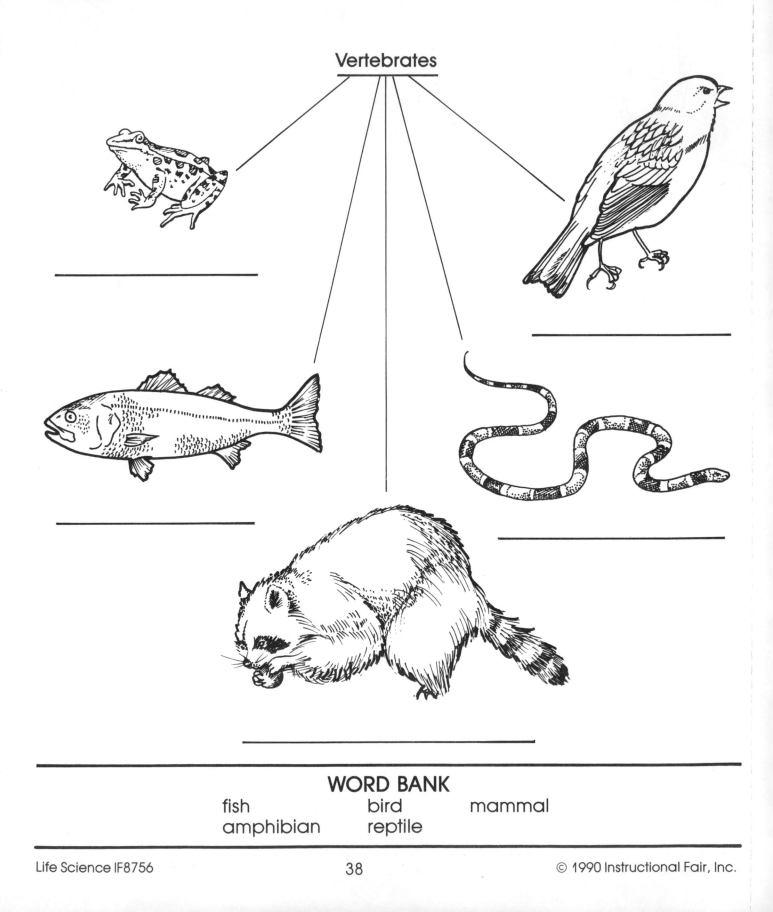

Vertebrates

_____

_____

_____

_____

_____

WORD BANK

fish	bird	mammal
amphibian	reptile	

38

Classy Vertebrates

Name _____

The vertebrates (chordates) are divided into **several different classes.**
Name the class for each vertebrate pictured below.

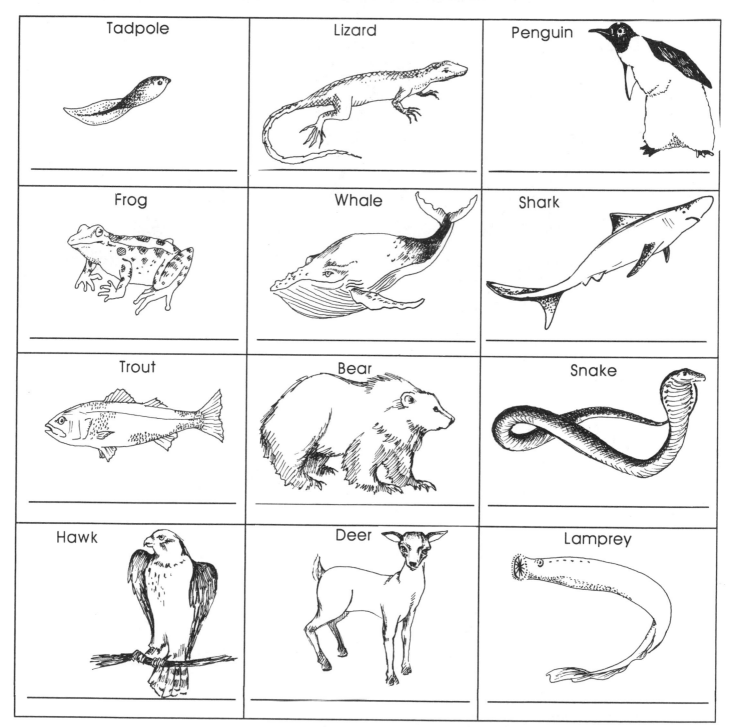

Tadpole

Lizard

Penguin

Frog

Whale

Shark

Trout

Bear

Snake

Hawk

Deer

Lamprey

WORD BANK

jawless fish	amphibians	birds
cartilage fish	reptiles	mammals
bony fish		

Backbones

Name _____

Animals with backbones are called vertebrates. Each of these vertebrates belongs to a different class.
Color the backbone in each of these skeletons. Write the class below each animal.

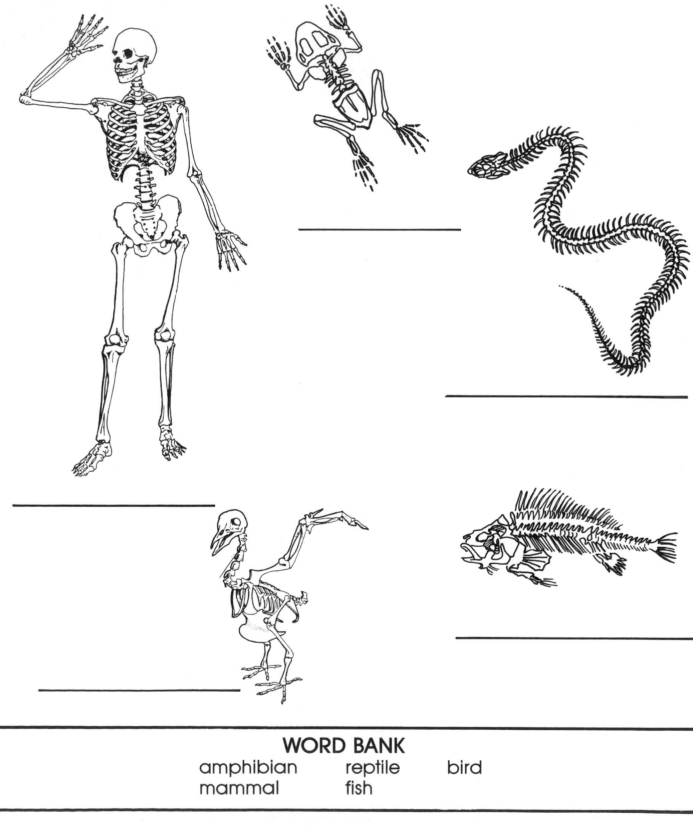

_____

_____

_____

_____

_____

WORD BANK

amphibian	reptile	bird
mammal	fish	

Animals with Backbones

Name _____

Vertebrates are animals that have backbones. They are members of a group called chordates.

Write the name of the class for each set of characteristics and an example of each.

Class	Characteristics	Example
	-skeleton of cartilage -paired fins -cold-blooded -toothlike scales on skin	
	-jawless -sucker-shaped mouth -cartilage skeleton -cold-blooded	
	-skeleton of bone -gill covers -scales -cold-blooded	
	-most young have gills -most adults have lungs -lay eggs in water or moist ground -cold-blooded	
	-dry, scaly skin -egg has tough shell -cold-blooded -well-developed lungs	
	-feathers -wings -hollow bones -warm-blooded	
	-hair at same point in life -feed milk to young -well-developed brain -warm-blooded	

WORD BANK

mammals	amphibians	shark	hawk	reptiles
bony fish	trout	bear	birds	cartilage fish
lizard	lamprey	jawless fish	frog	

Vertebrates

Vertebrates, animals with backbones, can be grouped **into several classes.**

List at least four characteristics for each of the classes below.

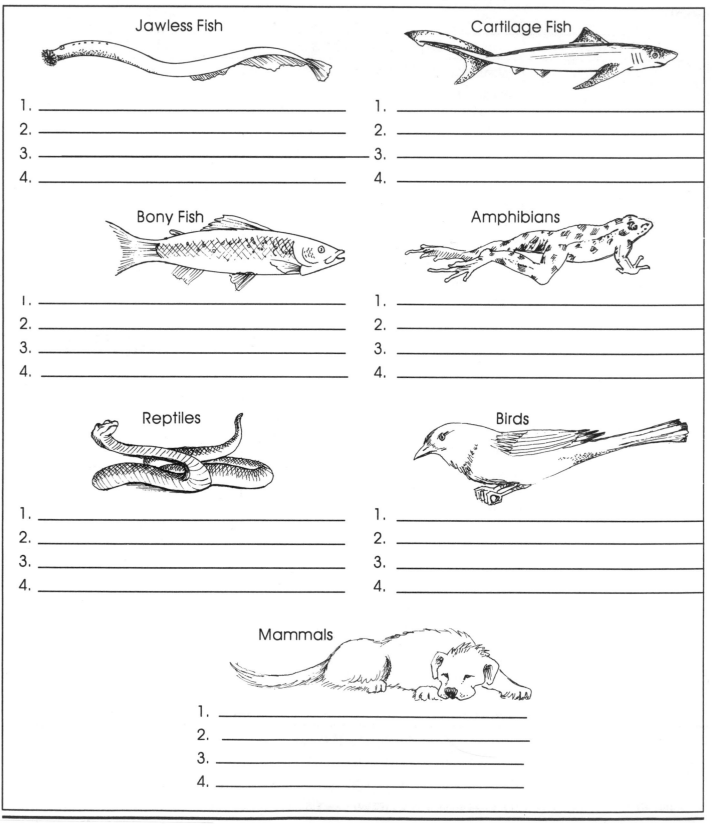

Jawless Fish

1. _____
2. _____
3. _____
4. _____

Cartilage Fish

1. _____
2. _____
3. _____
4. _____

Bony Fish

1. _____
2. _____
3. _____
4. _____

Amphibians

1. _____
2. _____
3. _____
4. _____

Reptiles

1. _____
2. _____
3. _____
4. _____

Birds

1. _____
2. _____
3. _____
4. _____

Mammals

1. _____
2. _____
3. _____
4. _____

Backbone or No Backbone?

Name _____

Animals with backbones are called vertebrates. Those without backbones are called invertebrates.
Label each animal as a vertebrate or invertebrate. Name each animal.

WORD BANK

horse	dog	cow	fish	clam
worm	fly	crayfish	bird	starfish

Rippers, Nippers and Grinders   Name _____

Most mammals have two or more types of teeth: **incisors** for nipping food like scissors; **canines** for tearing food; and **molars** for grinding food.

Label the teeth on these animals.

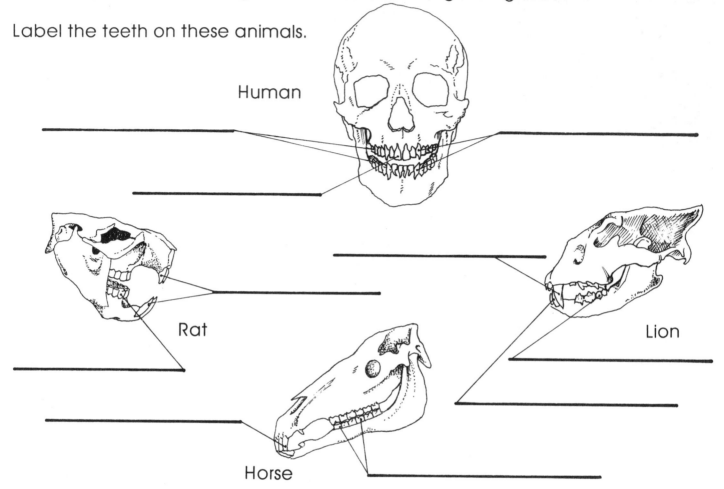

Human

Rat

Horse

Lion

Animal	Type of Teeth	Kinds of Food Eaten
Rat		
Lion		
Horse		
Human		

WORD BANK

incisors	molars	canines
grains	grasses	meats
vegetables	dairy products	fruits

44   © 1990 Instructional Fair, Inc.

The Mammal with Wings

Name _____

Unlike other mammals, bats have true wings. But bat's wings are also like arms. Label the parts of a bat.

WORD BANK

foot	tail	wing membrane
thumb	second finger	third finger
fourth finger	fifth finger	upper arm
forearm		

The Fish

Label the exterior parts of the fish.

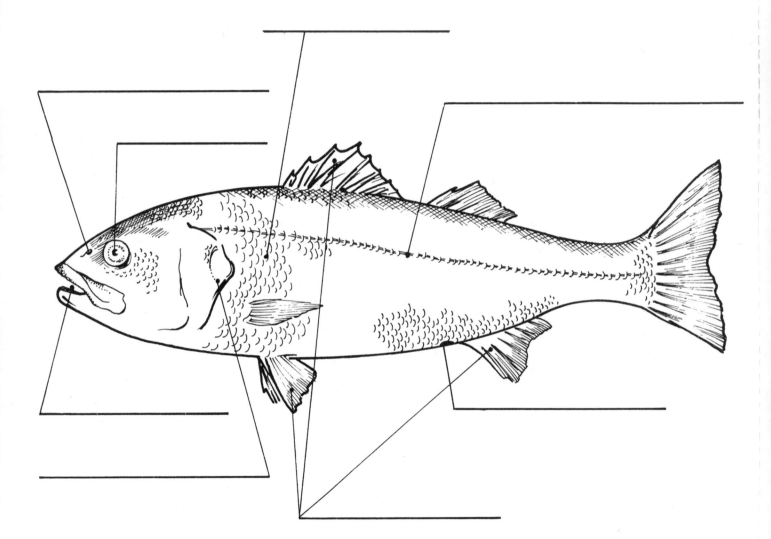

WORD BANK

| mouth | nostril | eye | scale |
| gill cover | fins | lateral line | anus |

The Fish – Internal

Name _____

Label the parts of the fish.

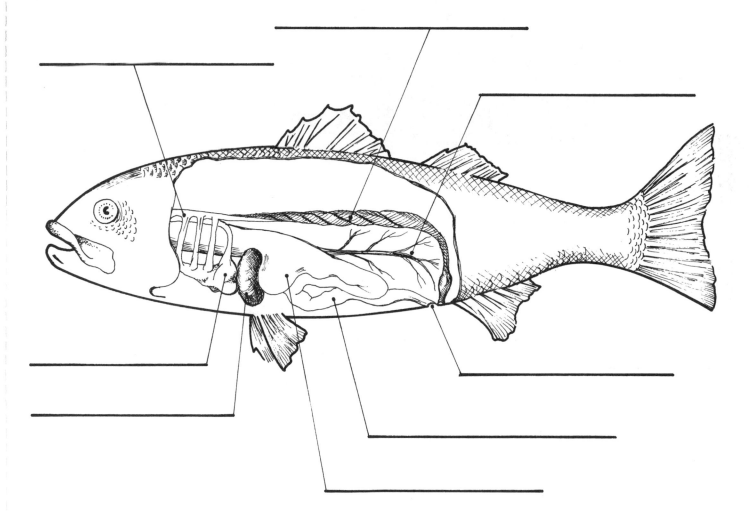

WORD BANK

dorsal aorta	kidney	stomach
ovary	anus	intestine
liver	heart	

The Frog

Name _____

Label the exterior parts of the frog and the parts of the frog's mouth.

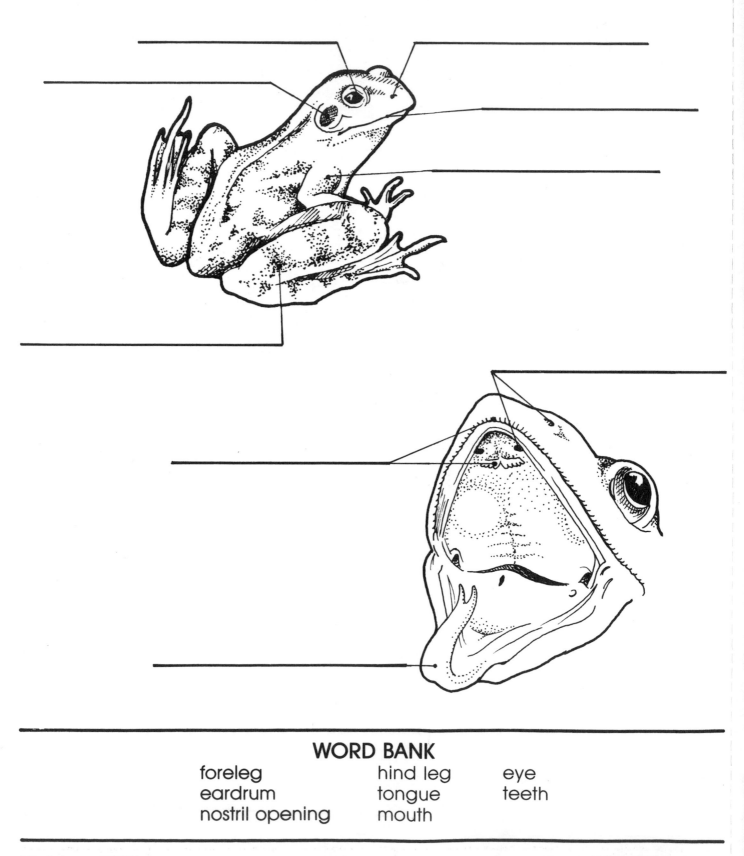

WORD BANK

foreleg	hind leg	eye
eardrum	tongue	teeth
nostril opening	mouth	

The Frog – Internal

Name _____

Label the parts of the frog.

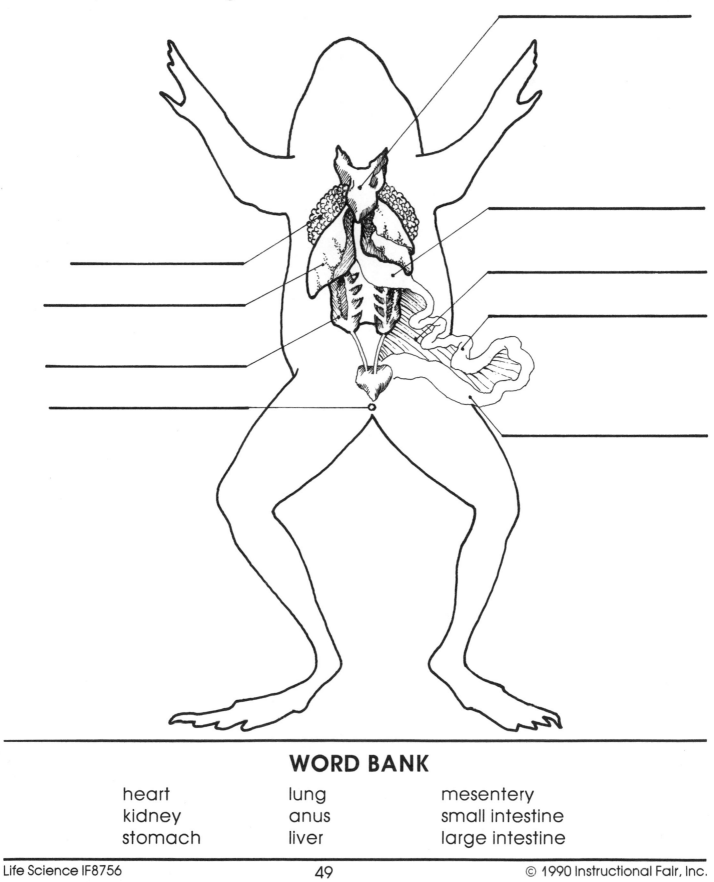

WORD BANK

heart	lung	mesentery
kidney	anus	small intestine
stomach	liver	large intestine

Life Cycle of a Frog

Label the steps in the life cycle of the frog.

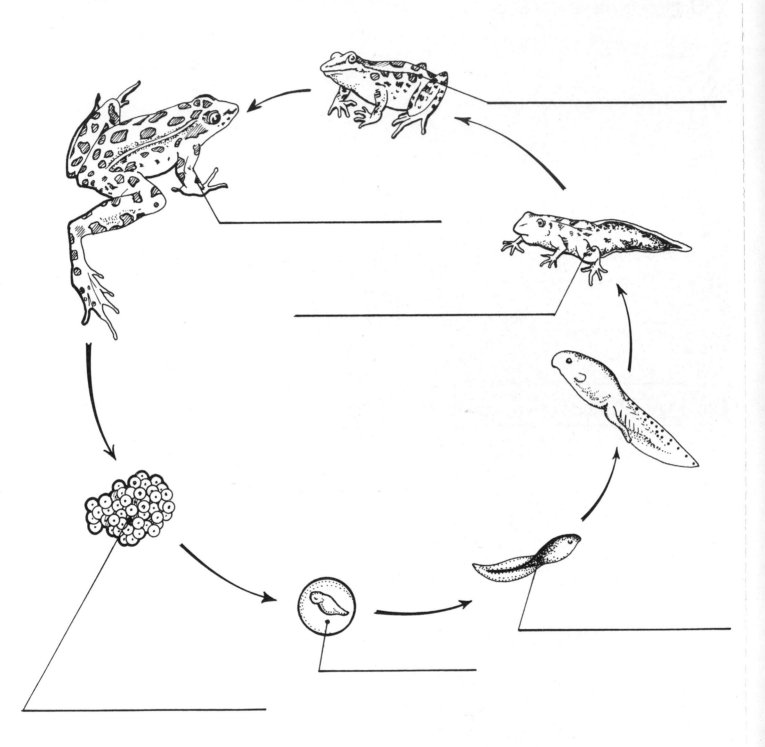

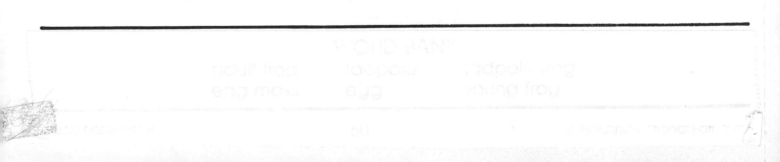

Pit Viper Snake

Name _____

Label the parts of the head of the pit viper snake.

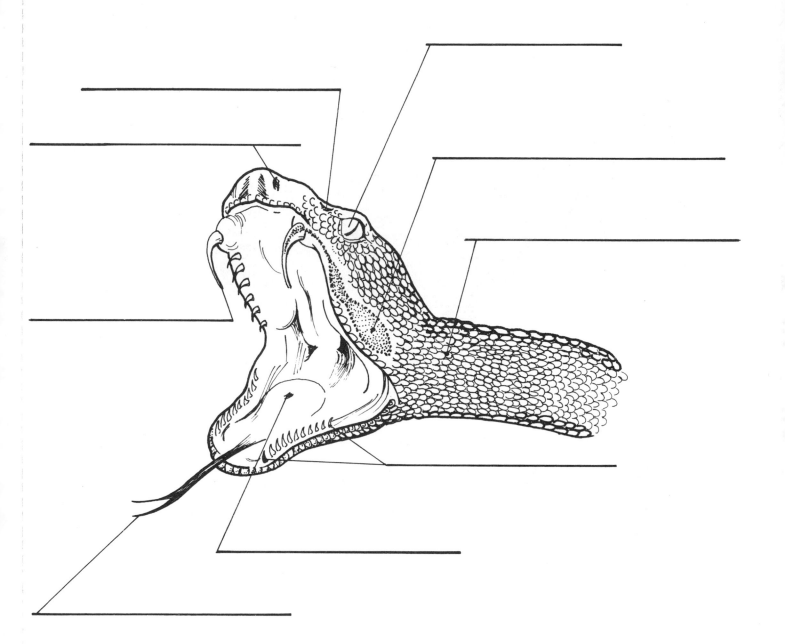

WORD BANK

eye	pit	nostril
fang	teeth	tongue
glottis (windpipe)	venom sac	scaly skin

The Parts of a Bird

Name _____

Field guides and other books often use special terms when describing a bird. Label the parts of the bird.

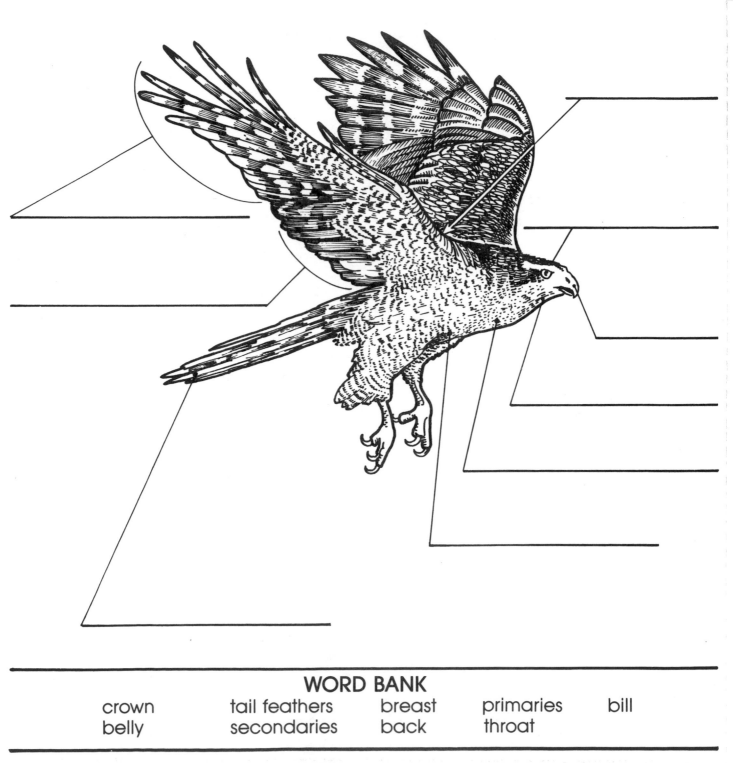

WORD BANK

crown	tail feathers	breast	primaries	bill
belly	secondaries	back	throat	

Feathers and Wings

Name _____

The wings and body of a bird are covered with different types of feathers.

Parts of a Wing
Label the three *groups* of feathers on the wing pictured below.

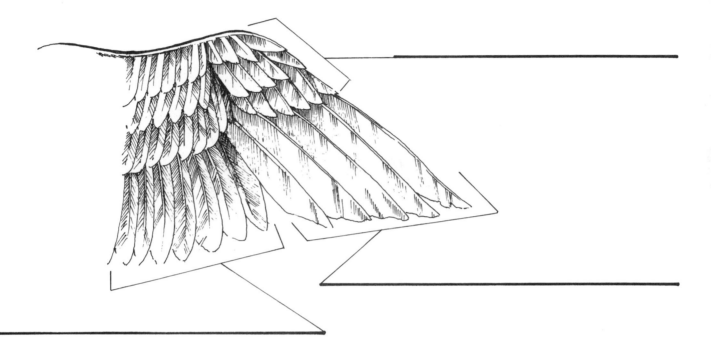

Feathers
Label the three *types* of feathers pictured below.

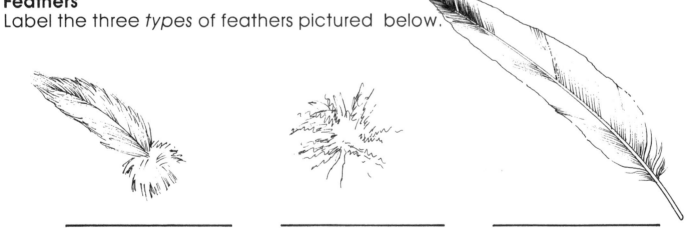

_____   _____   _____

WORD BANK

coverts   body feather
secondary flight feathers   down feather
primary flight feathers   primary flight feather

Bird Bones

Name _____

Label the major bone structures of a bird.

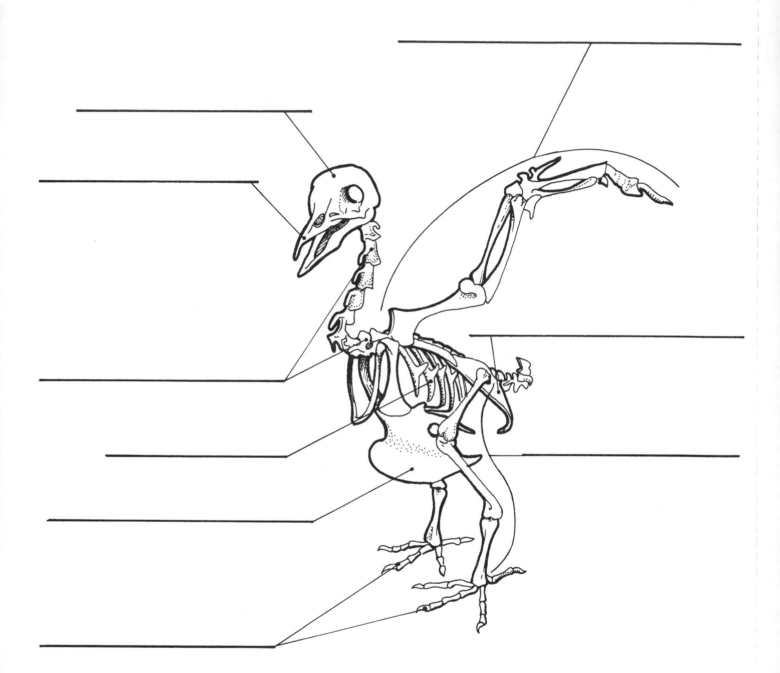

WORD BANK

wing bones	pelvic girdle	vertebrae
skull	beak	ribs
feet	leg bones	breastbone

Feathered Friend's Feet

Name _____

A bird's feet can tell you many things about its habits or home. How do each of these birds use their feet in a special way?

_____

_____

_____

_____

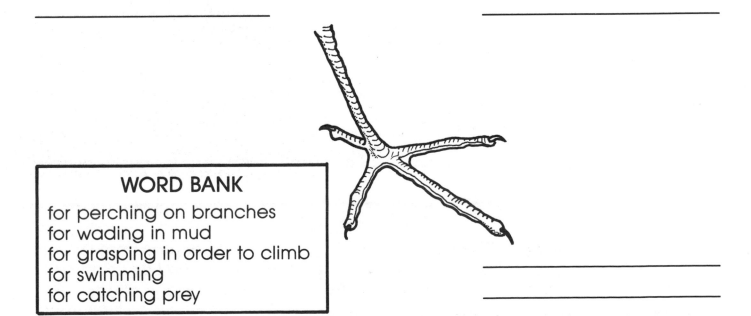

```
WORD BANK

for perching on branches
for wading in mud
for grasping in order to climb
for swimming
for catching prey
```

_____

Bird Bills

Name _____

The shape of a bird's bill can often tell what the bird eats. How do each of these birds use their bills in a special way to eat food?

_____   _____

_____   _____

_____   _____

_____   _____

_____   _____

WORD BANK

for pounding holes to find insects   to suck nectar from flowers
to tear the flesh of animals   to stab small fish
to scoop large mouthfuls of water and fish to crack open seeds

---

More Bird Bills

Name _____

The shape of a bird's bill will often tell what kind of food the bird eats.

Describe the feeding habits of each bird.

_____

_____

_____

_____

_____

_____

_____

_____

_____

_____

_____

_____

WORD BANK

cracks nuts and seeds
tears flesh
traps insects in midair
scoops fish from water

grabs and holds worms
sweeps back and forth through
water and filters out tiny plants
and animals

Strangers in the Night

Name _____

It's much easier to identify a bird when you can see its coloring, size and shape. At night this is usually difficult.

See if you can identify these birds by their silhouettes only.

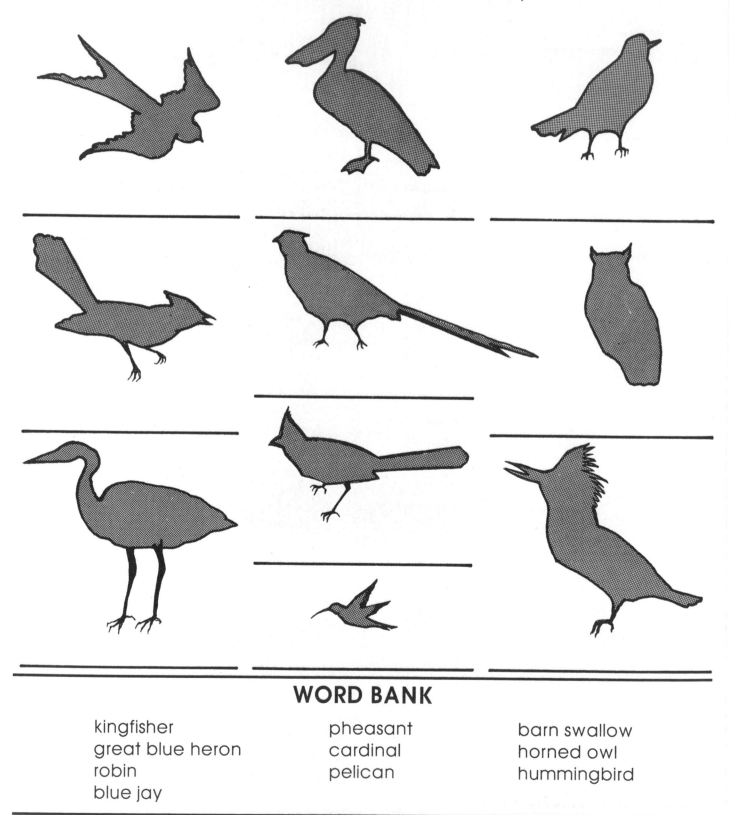

WORD BANK

kingfisher   pheasant   barn swallow
great blue heron   cardinal   horned owl
robin   pelican   hummingbird
blue jay

Highways for the Birds

Name _____

Label each of these major flyways found in North America.

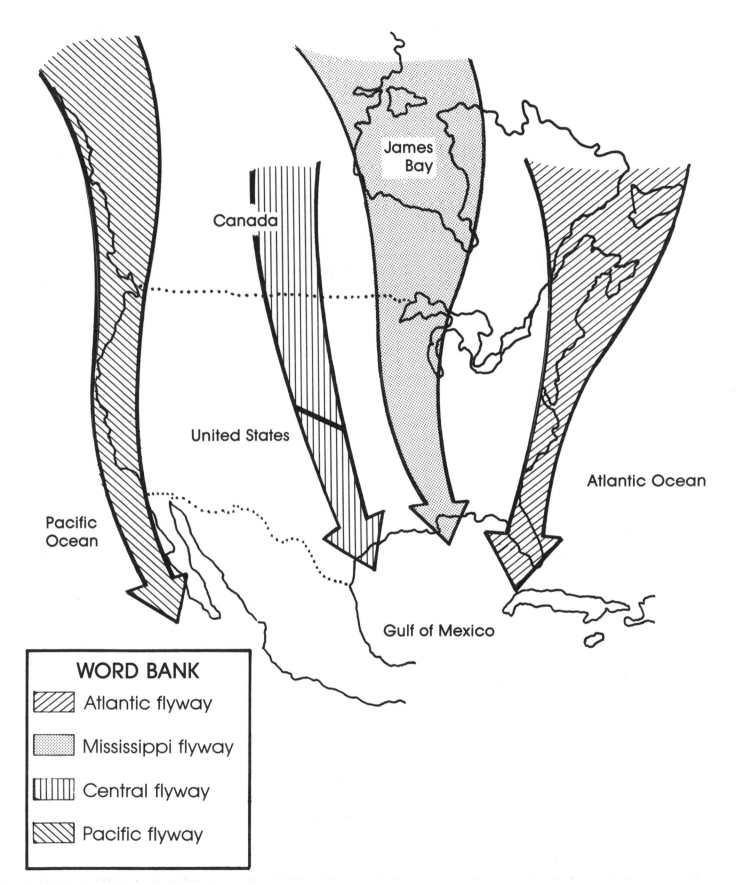

James Bay

Canada

United States

Atlantic Ocean

Pacific Ocean

Gulf of Mexico

WORD BANK

Atlantic flyway

Mississippi flyway

Central flyway

Pacific flyway

Bird Egg

Label the parts of the egg.

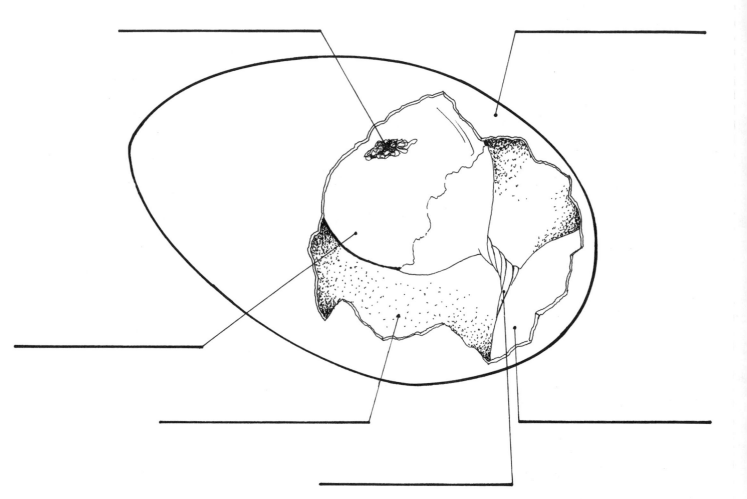

WORD BANK

germ	chalaza	shell
albumen	yolk	air space

Chicken Egg

Label the parts of this fertilized hen's egg.

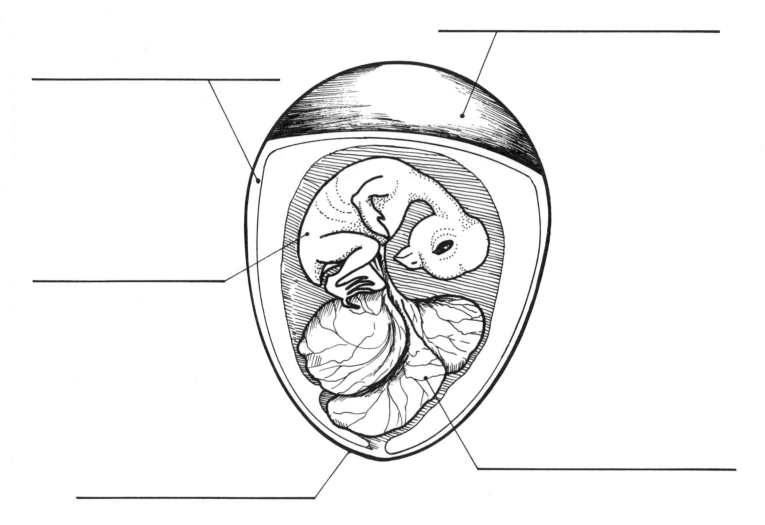

WORD BANK

| membrane | air space | embryo |
| yolk sac | shell | |

61

Classes of Arthropods

Name _____

Arthropods are animals that have jointed legs. Three-fourths of all the different animal types belong to this group.

Write the name of the class for each set of characteristics and an example of each.

Class	Characteristics	Example
	-round -segmented body -two pairs of legs per segment	
	-flat -segmented body -one pair of legs per segment	
	-hard -flexible exoskeleton -gills -two pairs of antennae -two body sections	
	-two body sections -no antennae -four pairs of legs	
	-three body sections -one pair of antennae -three pairs of legs	

WORD BANK

diplopoda   arachnida   centipede
chilopoda   insecta   lobster
crustacea   bee   spider
millipede

     62

The Crayfish

Name _____

Label the parts of the crayfish.

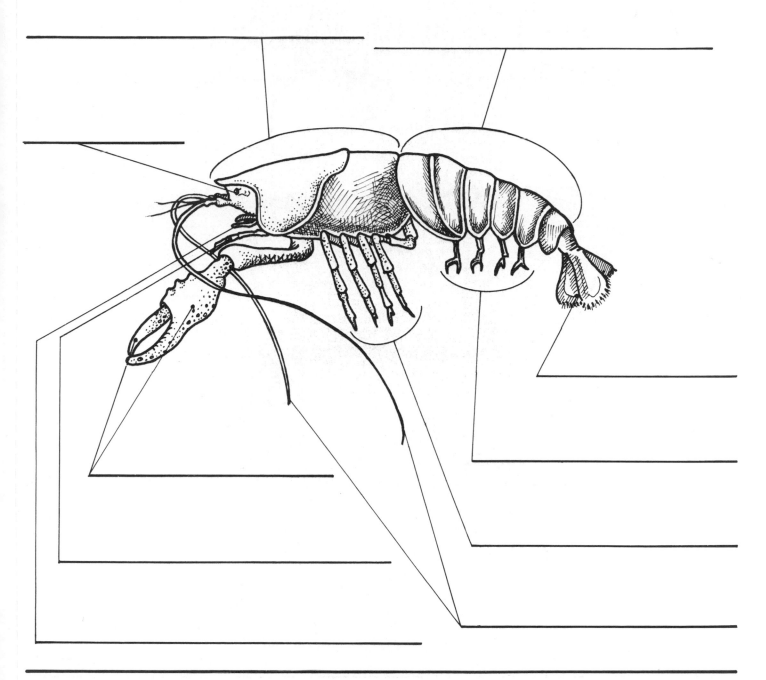

WORD BANK

eye	walking legs	flipper
swimmerets	abdomen	antennae
cephalothorax	cheliped	maxilliped
mandible		

Insect Orders

Name _____

The major groups of insects are called orders. Below are examples from seven of the most common orders of insects. Label each insect and its order.

_____

_____

_____

_____

_____

_____

_____

_____

_____

_____

_____

_____

_____

_____

WORD BANK

beetles (Coleoptera)

flies (Diptera)

grasshoppers (Orthoptera)

leafhoppers (Homoptera)

bees and wasps (Hymenoptera)

butterflies and moths (Lepidoptera)

true bugs (Hemiptera)

Orderly Insects

Name —————————

There are more than twenty-five different orders of insects. Seven of the most common orders are listed below.

Write the name of the insects pictured under the correct order.

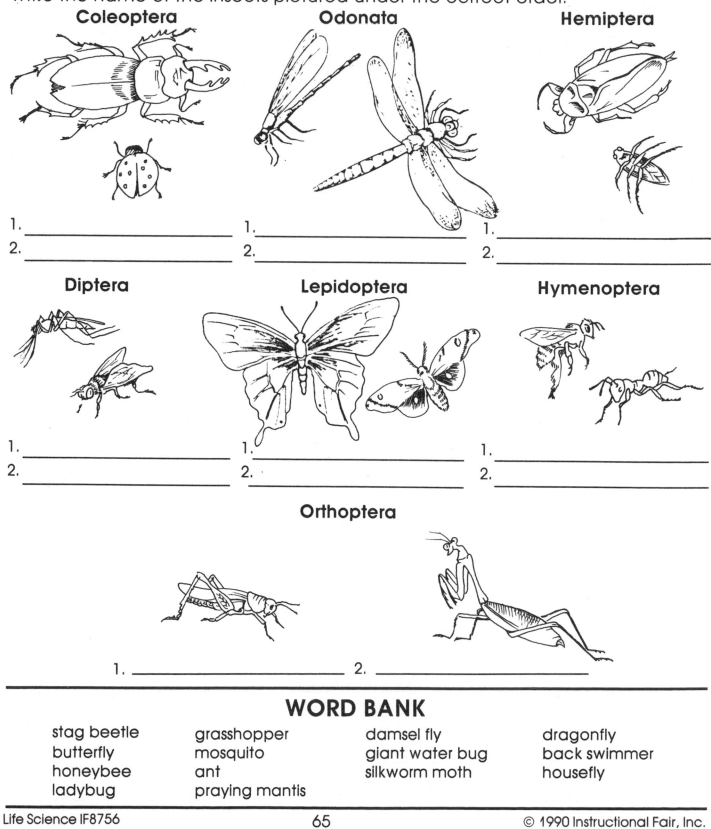

Coleoptera

1. _____
2. _____

Odonata

1. _____
2. _____

Hemiptera

1. _____
2. _____

Diptera

1. _____
2. _____

Lepidoptera

1. _____
2. _____

Hymenoptera

1. _____
2. _____

Orthoptera

1. _____   2. _____

WORD BANK

stag beetle	grasshopper	damsel fly	dragonfly
butterfly	mosquito	giant water bug	back swimmer
honeybee	ant	silkworm moth	housefly
ladybug	praying mantis		

Spiders and Insects

Name _____

Spiders are not insects. Label the parts of the spider and insect.

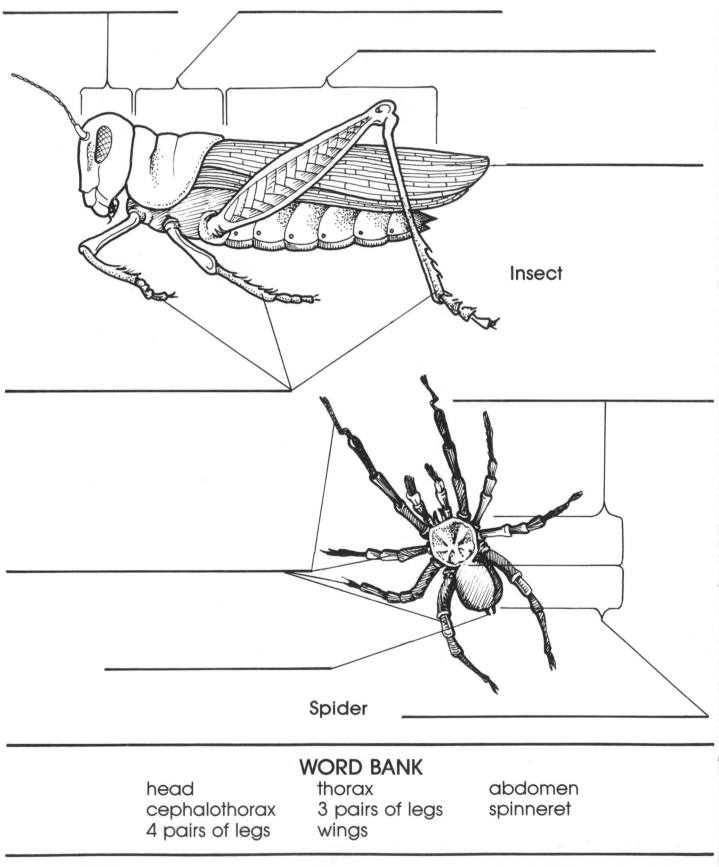

Insect

Spider

WORD BANK

head	thorax	abdomen
cephalothorax	3 pairs of legs	spinneret
4 pairs of legs	wings	

Common Water Insects

Name _____

Identify these common water insects.

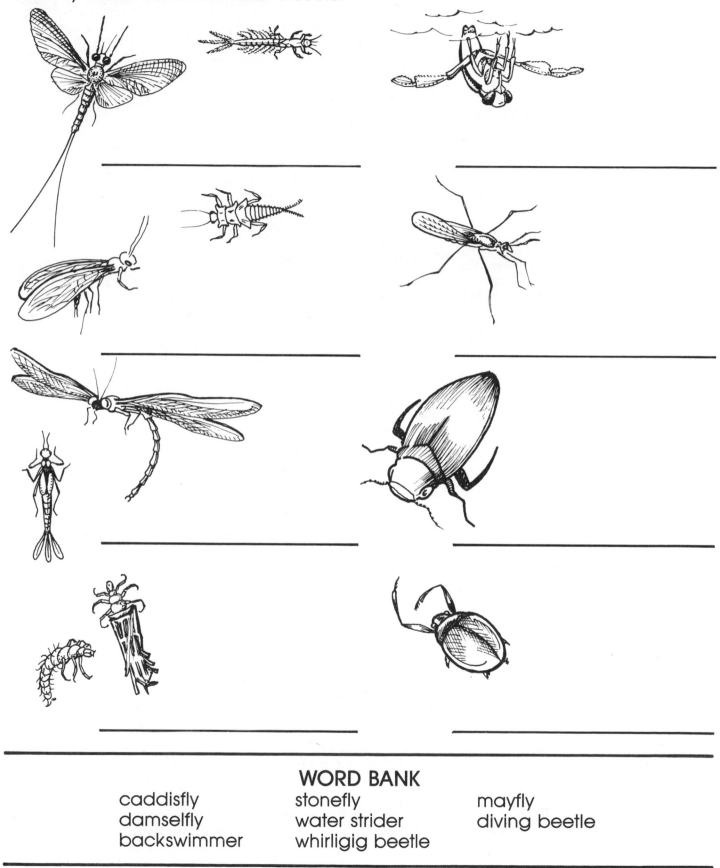

WORD BANK

caddisfly	stonefly	mayfly
damselfly	water strider	diving beetle
backswimmer	whirligig beetle	

The Worker Bee

Name _____

Label the parts of the worker bee.

WORD BANK

antenna	thorax	wing
abdomen	antenna cleaner	pollen combs
pollen basket	stinger	wax scales
spurs		

The Life Cycle of a Bee

Name _____

Label the stages of a bee's life cycle.

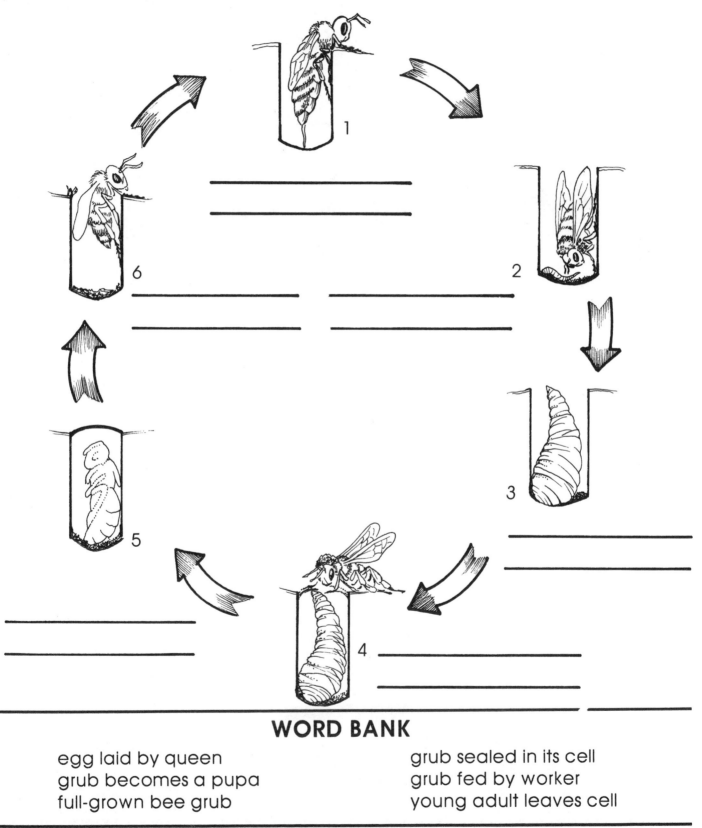

WORD BANK

egg laid by queen
grub becomes a pupa
full-grown bee grub

grub sealed in its cell
grub fed by worker
young adult leaves cell

The Ant

Name _____

Label the parts of the ant's body.

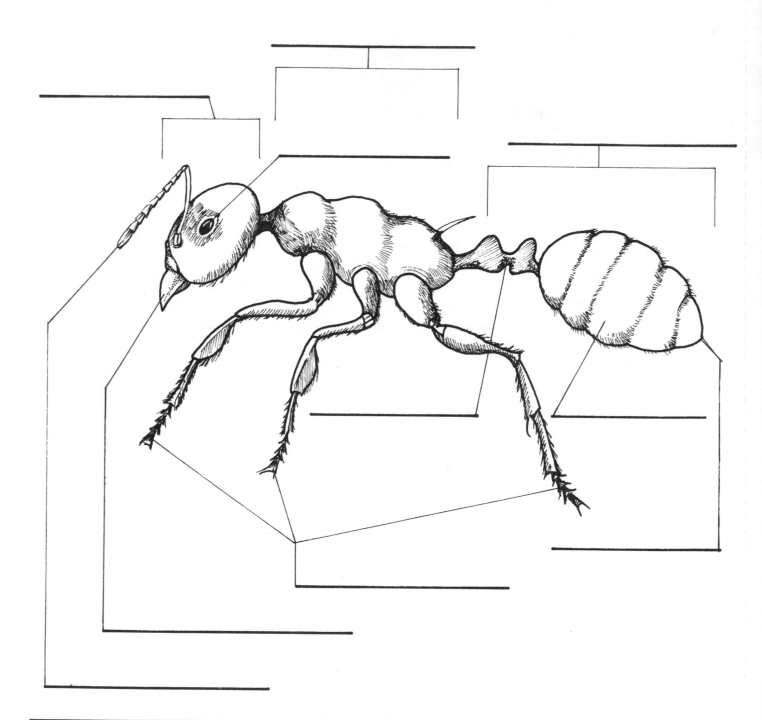

WORD BANK

head	trunk	metasoma
antenna	mandibles	eye
legs	gaster	sting
waist		

The Life Cycle of an Ant

Name _____

Label the four stages of an ant's life cycle.

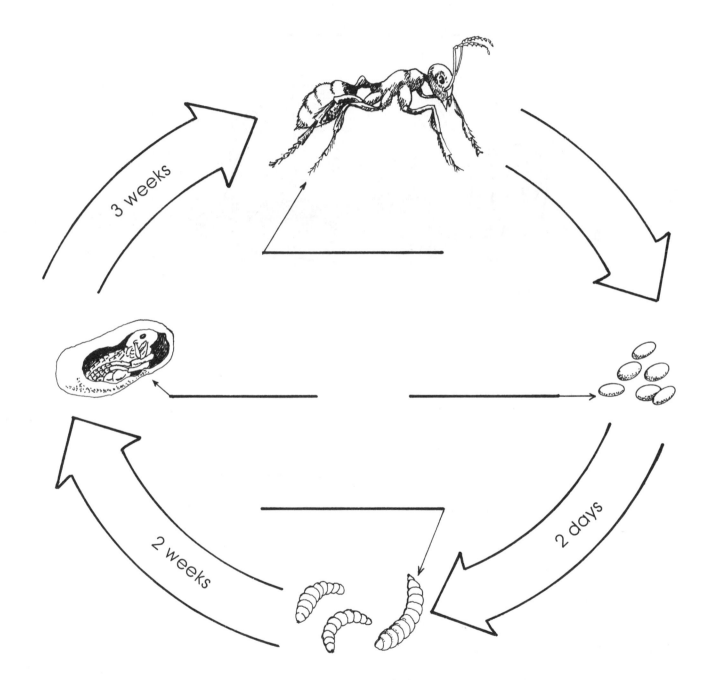

WORD BANK

eggs   adult   larvae   pupa

The Grasshopper

Label the parts of the grasshopper.

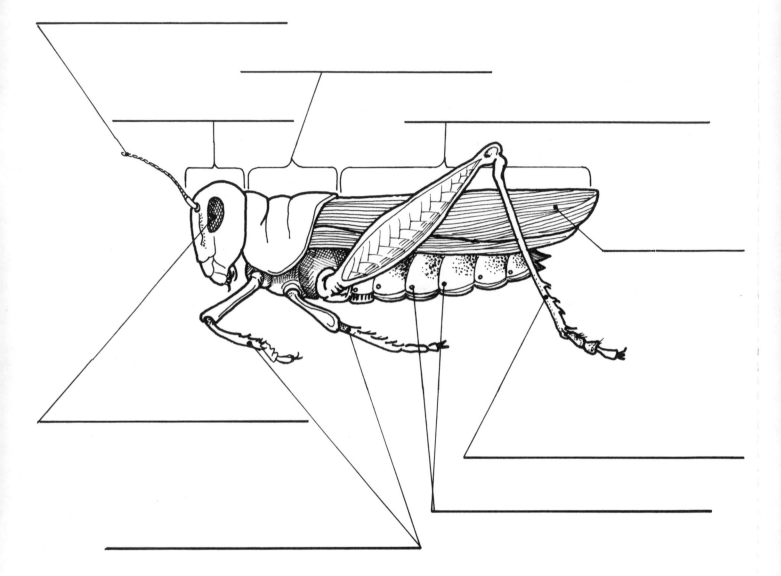

WORD BANK

head	thorax	abdomen
antenna	compound eye	walking legs
jumping leg	wing	spiracles

    72

The Grasshopper's Life Cycle

Name _____

The grasshopper's life cycle is an example of gradual metamorphosis. Label the steps of this cycle.

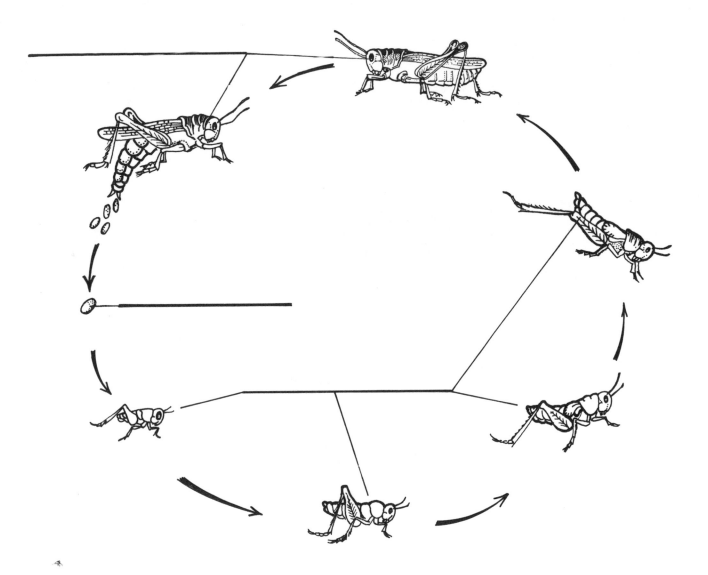

WORD BANK

adult   egg   nymph

Butterflies and Moths

Butterflies and moths belong to the order of insects called Lepidoptera. Moths and butterflies each have some special characteristics to help you tell them apart. Label the parts of the butterfly. Label the special characteristics as either butterfly or moth.

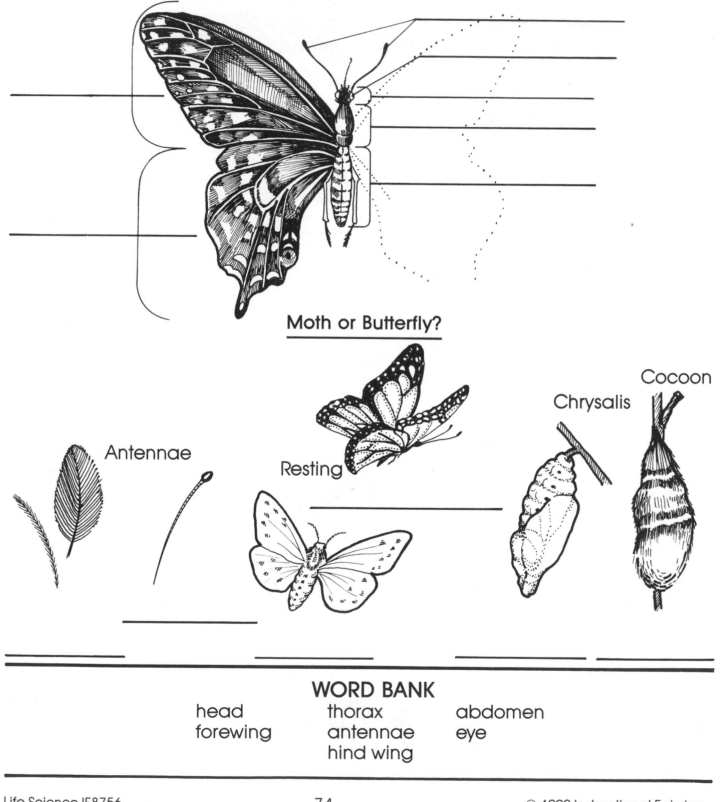

Moth or Butterfly?

Antennae

Resting

Chrysalis

Cocoon

WORD BANK

head	thorax	abdomen
forewing	antennae	eye
	hind wing	

The Monarch's Life Cycle

Name _____

The life cycle of a monarch butterfly is an example of complete metamorphosis. Label the steps in this life cycle.

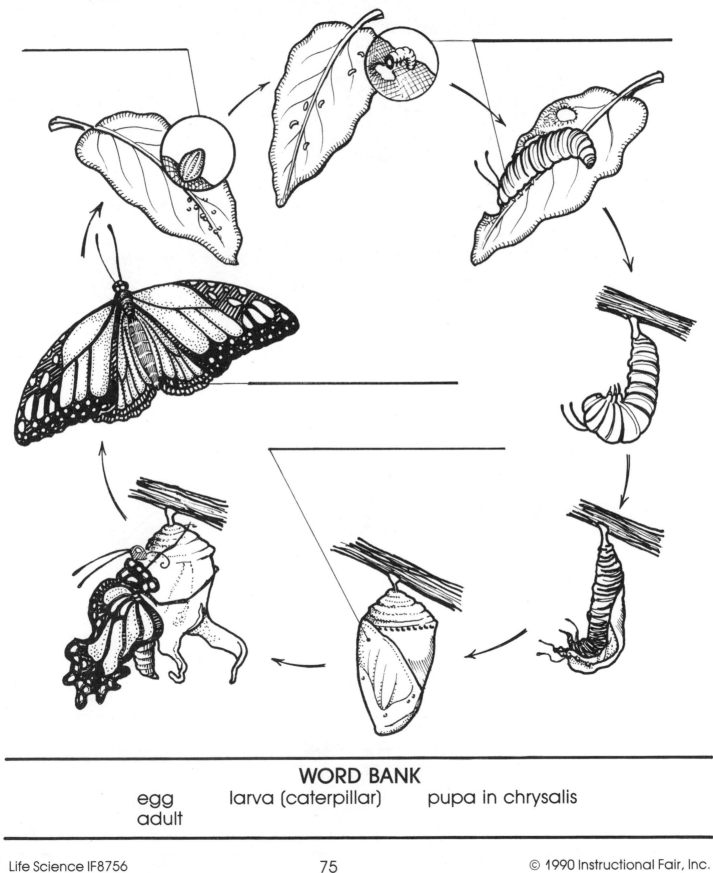

WORD BANK

egg   larva (caterpillar)   pupa in chrysalis
adult

Metamorphosis

Name _____

Label the stages of Complete and Incomplete Metamorphosis.

_____ Metamorphosis

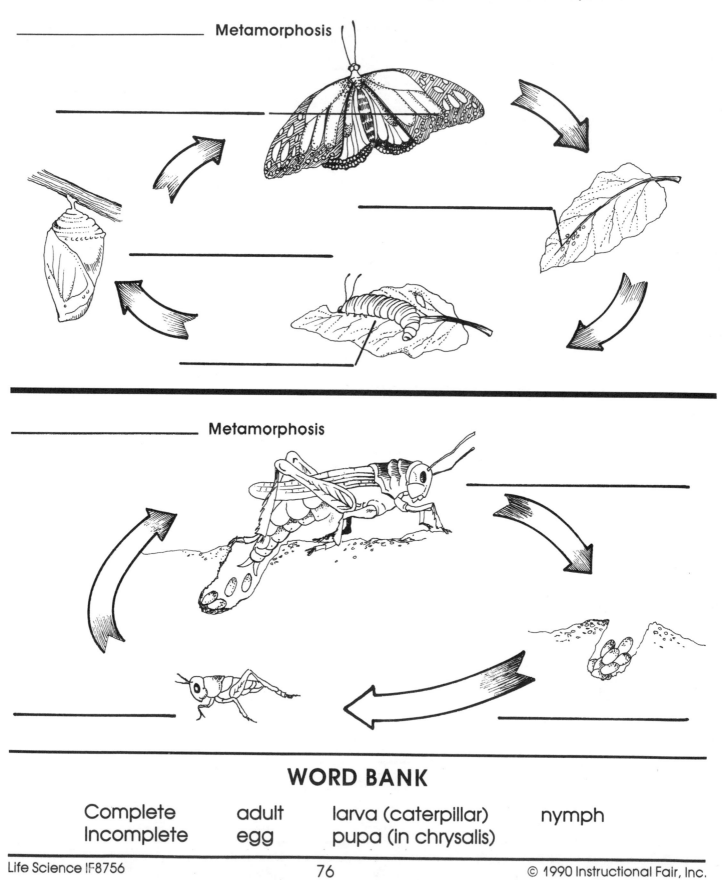

_____ Metamorphosis

WORD BANK

Complete	adult	larva (caterpillar)	nymph
Incomplete	egg	pupa (in chrysalis)	

The Clam

Label the parts of the clam.

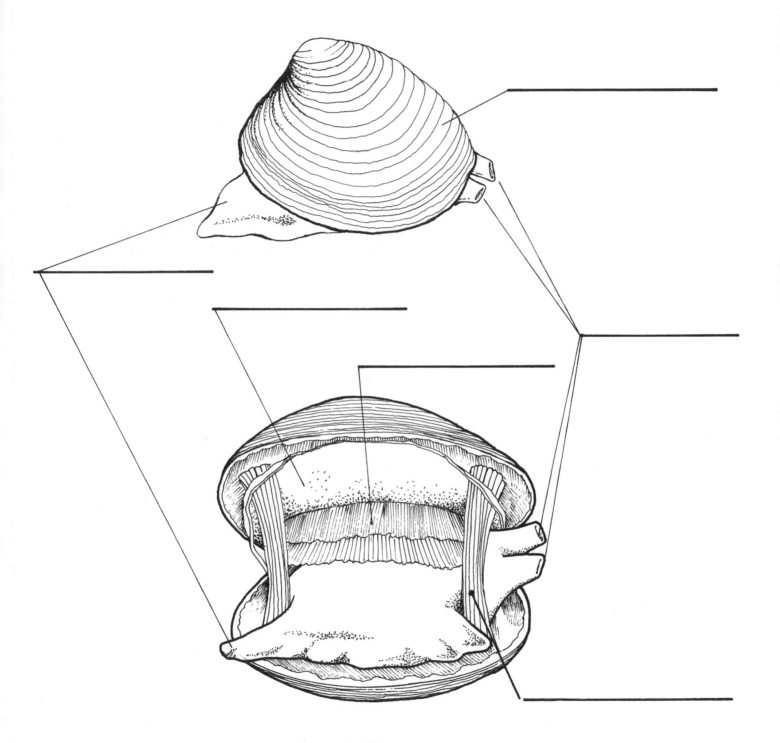

WORD BANK

| shell | gills | siphons |
| foot | muscle | mantle |

The Starfish

Name _____

Label the parts of the starfish.

_____

_____

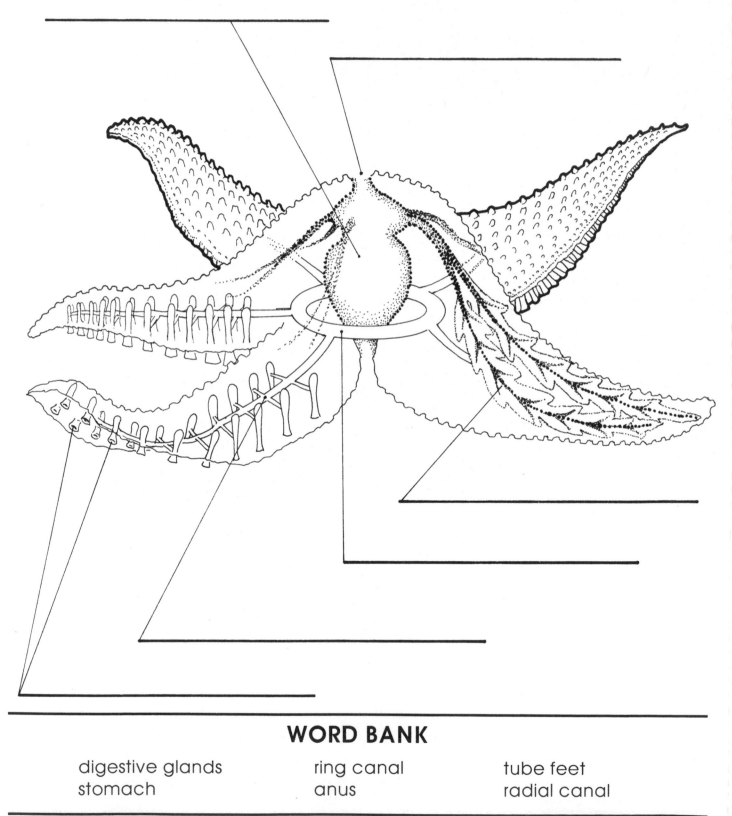

_____

_____

_____

WORD BANK

digestive glands	ring canal	tube feet
stomach	anus	radial canal

The Sponge

Name _____

Label the parts of the sponge.

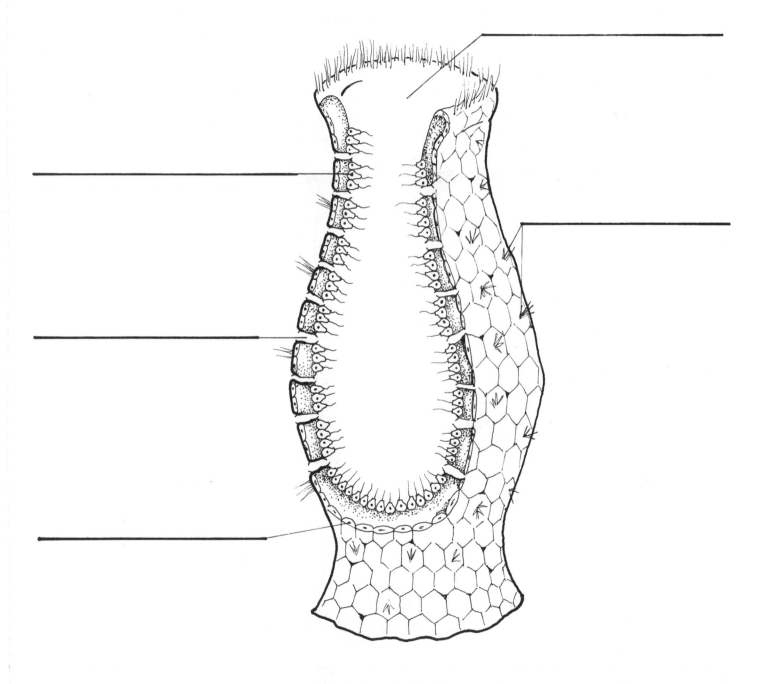

WORD BANK

osculum	spicule	pore
collar cell	epidermal cell	

The Hydra

Label the parts of the hydra.

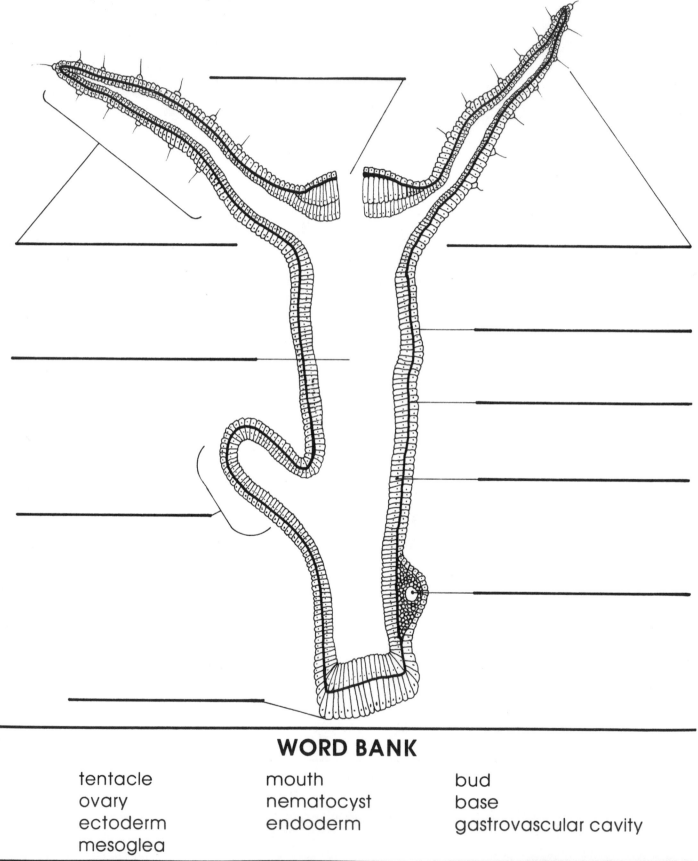

WORD BANK

tentacle   mouth   bud
ovary   nematocyst   base
ectoderm   endoderm   gastrovascular cavity
mesoglea

The Planarian

A planarian is a small flatworm that can regenerate missing body parts when portions are cut off.

Label the parts of the regenerated planarian.

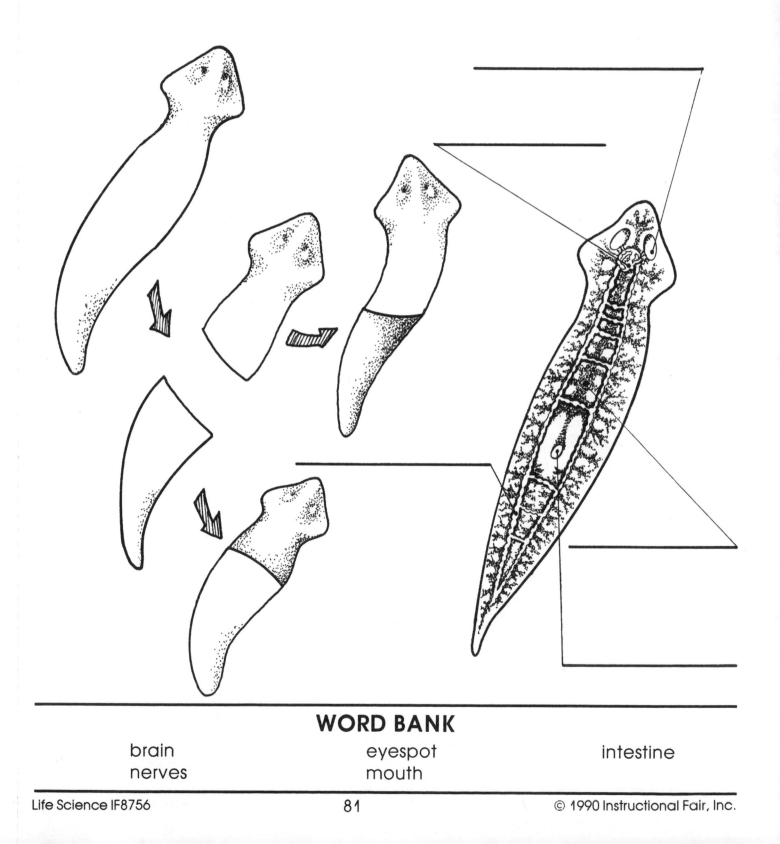

WORD BANK

brain   eyespot   intestine
nerves   mouth

Worms

There are thousands of different kinds of worms. Each kind belongs to one of the four major groups of worms.

Draw a line from each pictured worm to the group to which it belongs.

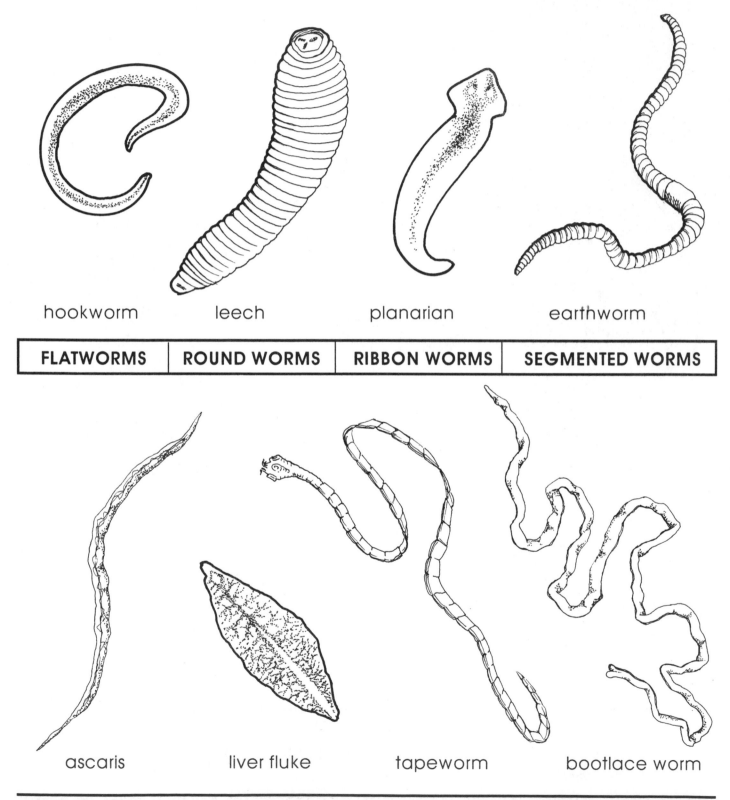

hookworm   leech   planarian   earthworm

FLATWORMS	ROUND WORMS	RIBBON WORMS	SEGMENTED WORMS

ascaris   liver fluke   tapeworm   bootlace worm

Worms, Cont'd

A key is a tool used by scientists to help them identify living things.

Use the key below to identify the worms on this page.

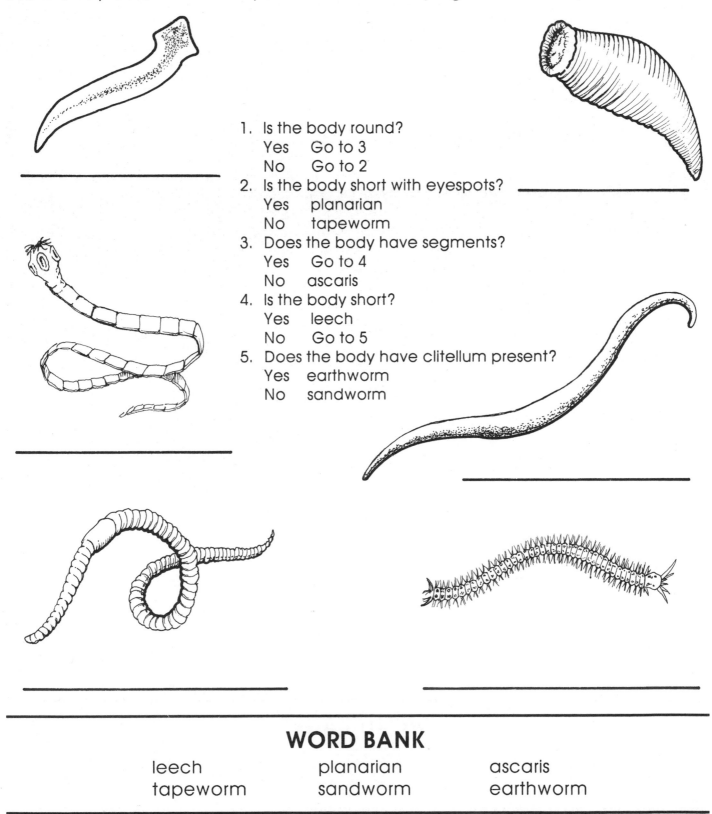

1. Is the body round?
   Yes   Go to 3
   No   Go to 2
2. Is the body short with eyespots?
   Yes   planarian
   No   tapeworm
3. Does the body have segments?
   Yes   Go to 4
   No   ascaris
4. Is the body short?
   Yes   leech
   No   Go to 5
5. Does the body have clitellum present?
   Yes   earthworm
   No   sandworm

WORD BANK

| leech | planarian | ascaris |
| tapeworm | sandworm | earthworm |

The Earthworm

Name _____

Label the exterior parts of the earthworm.

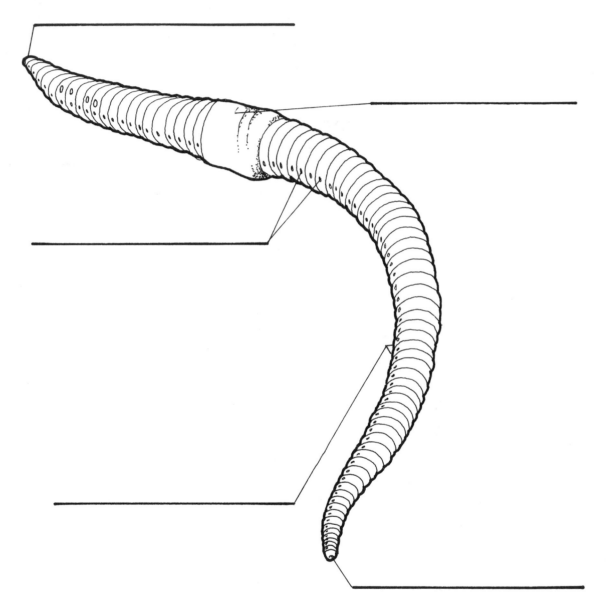

WORD BANK

mouth	clitellum	setae
segment	anus	

The Earthworm – Circulatory System

Name _____

The earthworm's circulatory system is very simple.

Label the parts of the earthworm and its circulatory system.

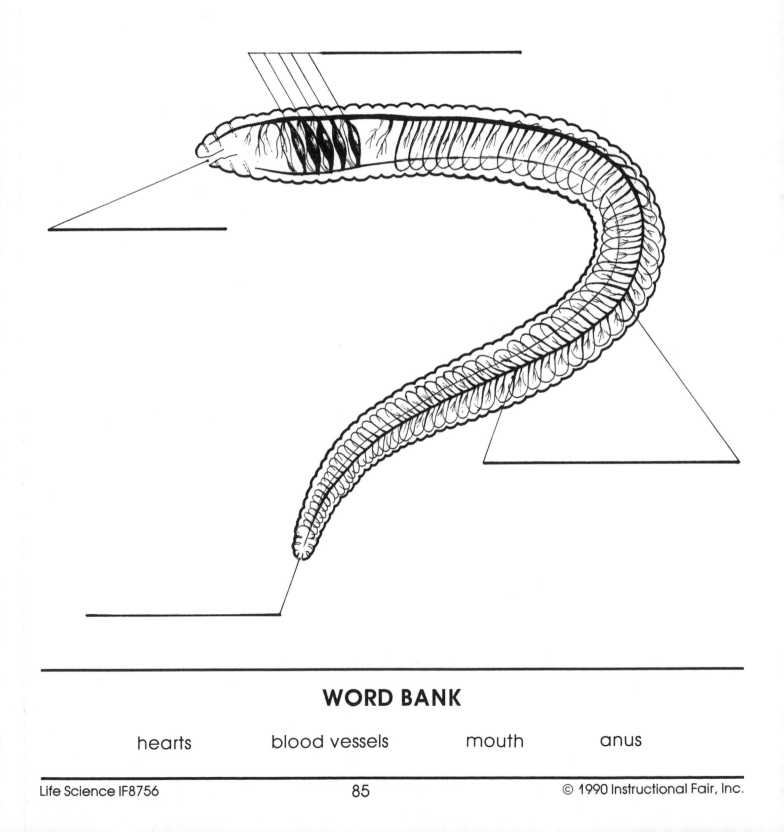

WORD BANK

hearts   blood vessels   mouth   anus

The Earthworm –
Digestive System

For the earthworm, as with most animals, digestion takes place in a long tube with openings at both ends. This tube is divided into organs that do different jobs.

Label the parts of the earthworm's digestive system.

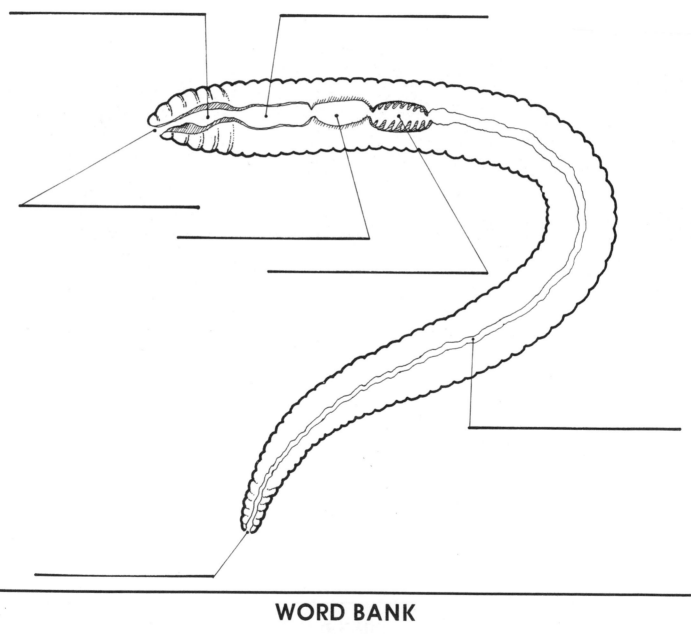

WORD BANK

crop	intestine	esophagus
mouth	gizzard	anus
pharynx		

Plant and Animal Cells

Name _____

Plant and animal cells are alike in many ways. But there are also ways in which they differ. Label the parts of the plant and animal cells.

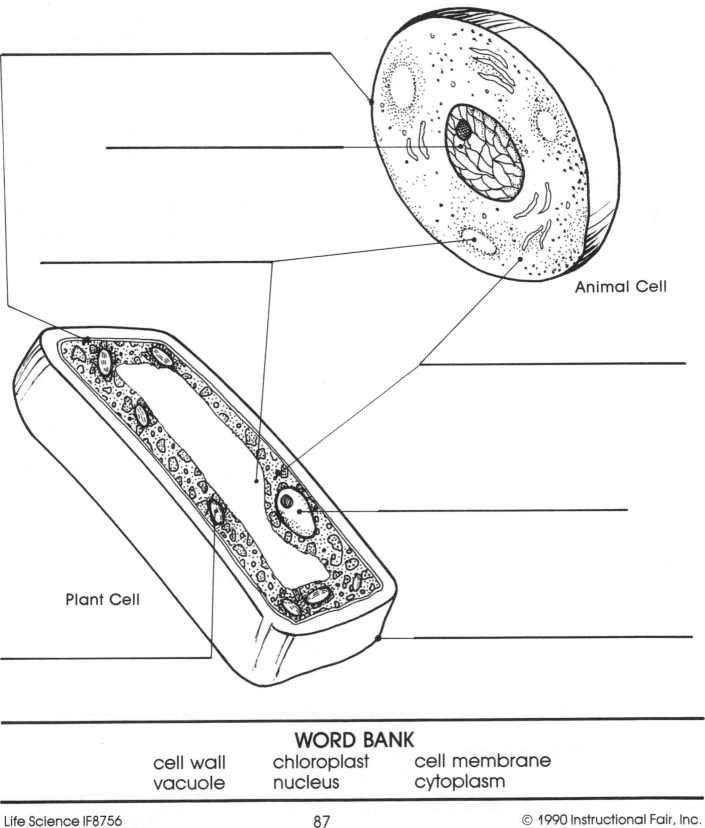

Animal Cell

Plant Cell

WORD BANK

| cell wall | chloroplast | cell membrane |
| vacuole | nucleus | cytoplasm |

The Amoeba

Label the parts of the reproducing amoeba.

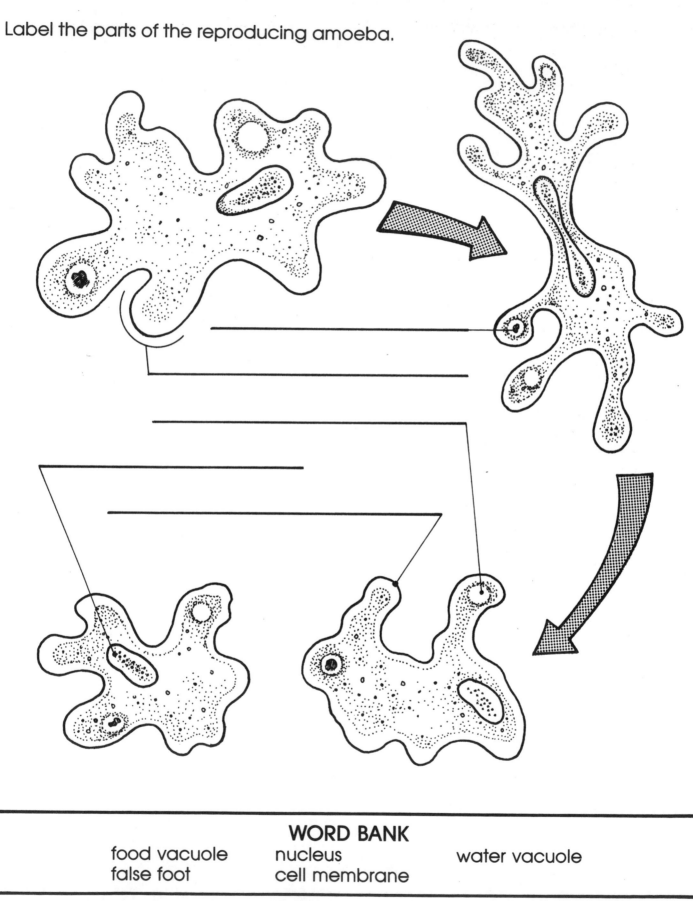

WORD BANK

food vacuole   nucleus   water vacuole
false foot   cell membrane

The Euglena

Name _____

Label the parts of the euglena.

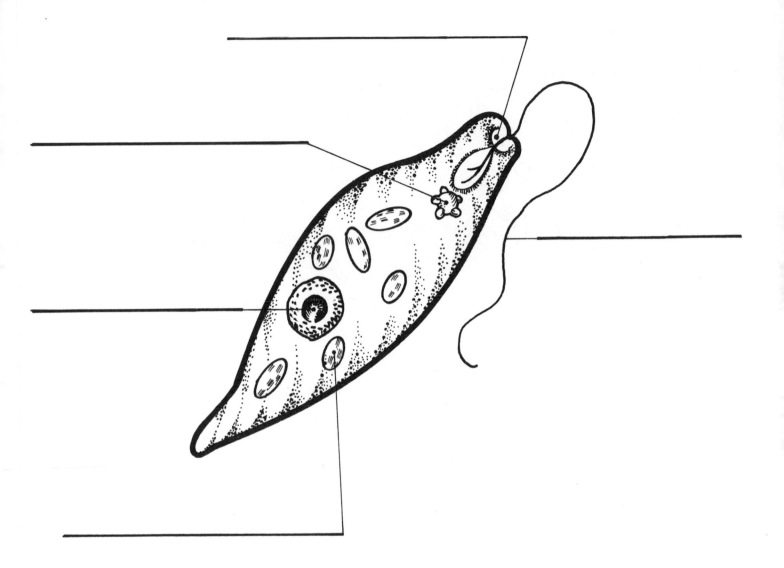

WORD BANK

| nucleus | chloroplast | contractile vacuole |
| eye spot | flagellum | |

The Paramecium

Name _____

Label the parts of the reproducing paramecium.

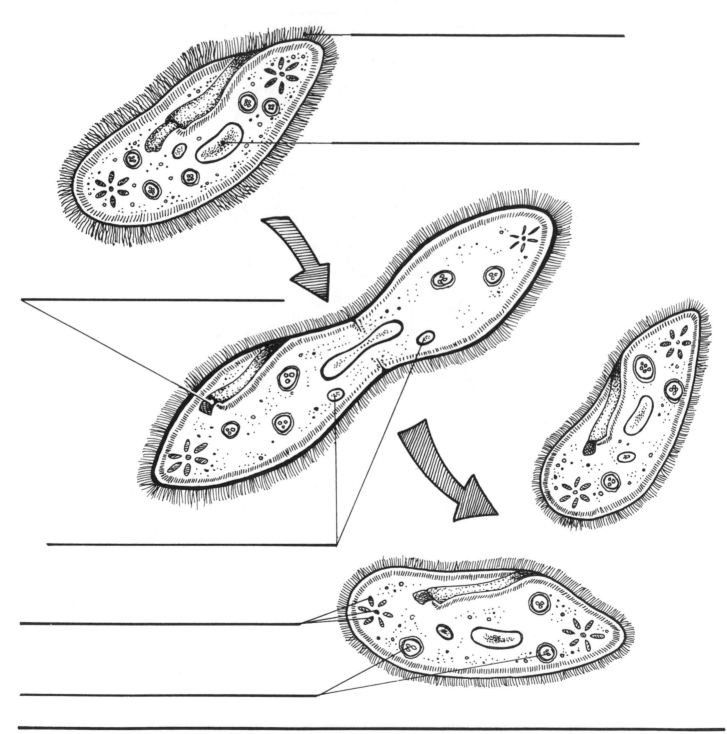

WORD BANK

food vacuoles	cilia	mouth opening
small nuclei	large nucleus	contractile vacuoles

The Growth of a Yeast Cell

Name _____

Label the parts of this growing yeast cell. Number the steps in the correct order.

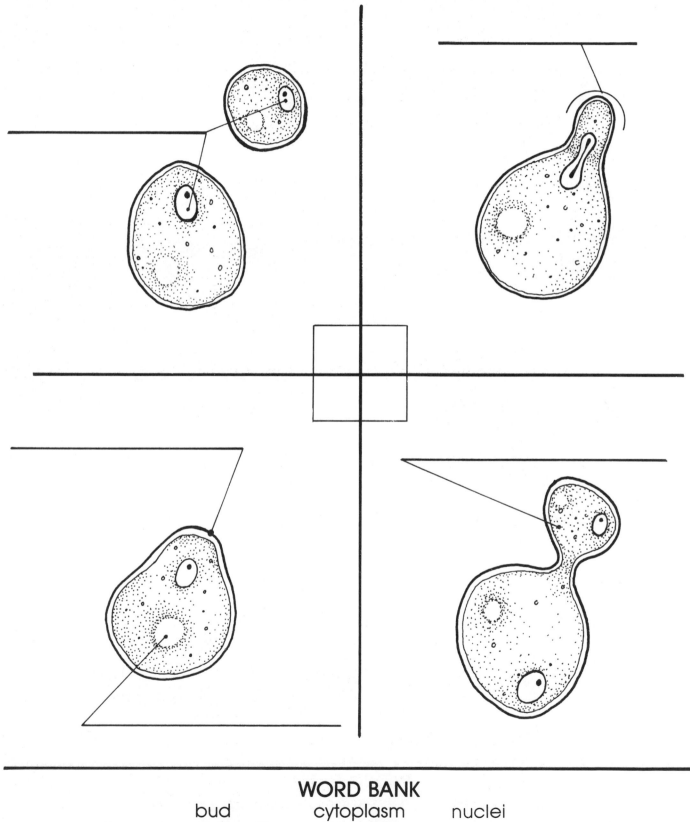

WORD BANK

bud   cytoplasm   nuclei
cell wall   vacuole

Food Chains

Name _____

The organisms found in a typical food chain are pictured below. Draw arrows from one organism to the next showing the order of the food chain. Write the name of each organism in the spaces.

WORD BANK

grass   grasshopper   frog
fish   man

Find the Missing Link

Write the missing organism in each food chain.

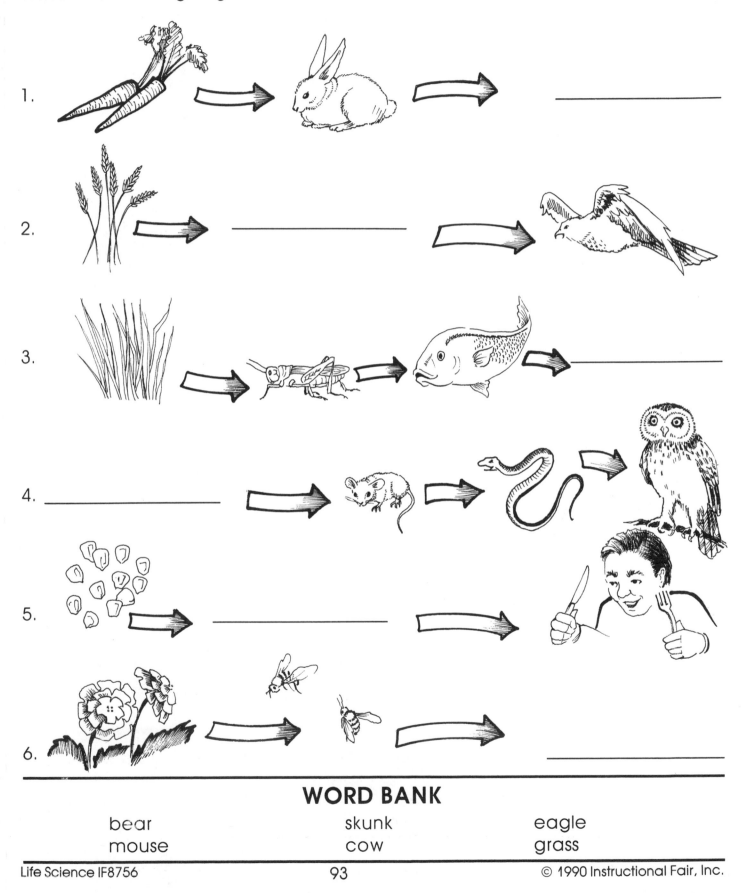

1.

2.

3.

4. _____

5.

6. _____

WORD BANK

bear	skunk	eagle
mouse	cow	grass

Producers and Consumers

Name _____

Organisms are either producers or consumers, depending upon the source of their energy. Consumers are either herbivores, carnivores or omnivores. Label the producers, omnivores, herbivores and carnivores in each food chain.

_____   _____   _____

_____   _____   _____

WORD BANK

carnivore   herbivore   omnivore
producer

Food Web

The organisms found in a typical food web are pictured below. Using arrows construct a food web. Label the organisms found in the food web.

WORD BANK

insect	frog	snake
trout	wolf	raccoon
mouse	deer	grass

95

Energy Pyramid

Name _____

Write the names of the organisms pictured on this page where they belong on the energy pyramid. Some may be listed on more than one level.

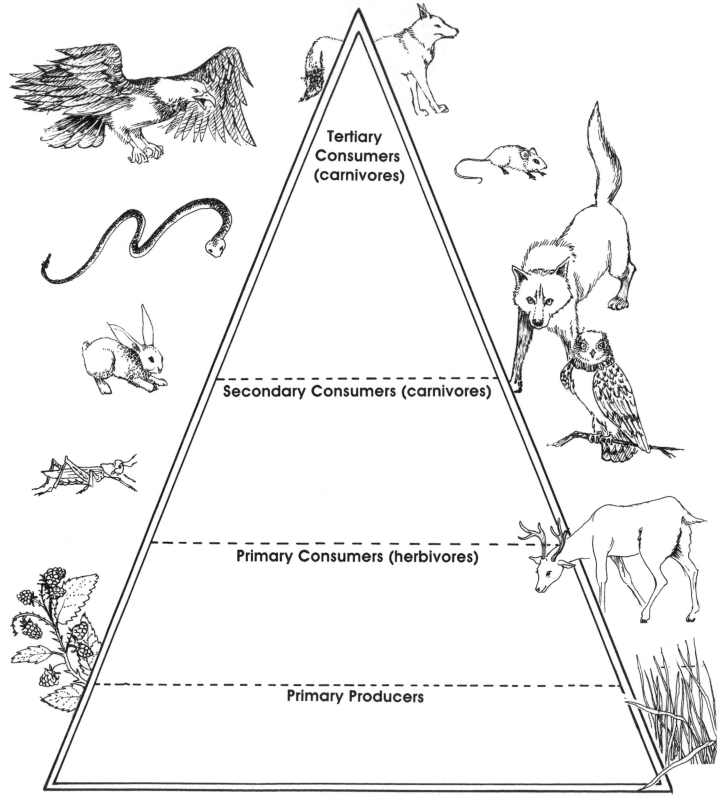

Tertiary
Consumers
(carnivores)

Secondary Consumers (carnivores)

Primary Consumers (herbivores)

Primary Producers

Biomes of North America

Name _____

Color the map and key to identify the major biomes of North America.

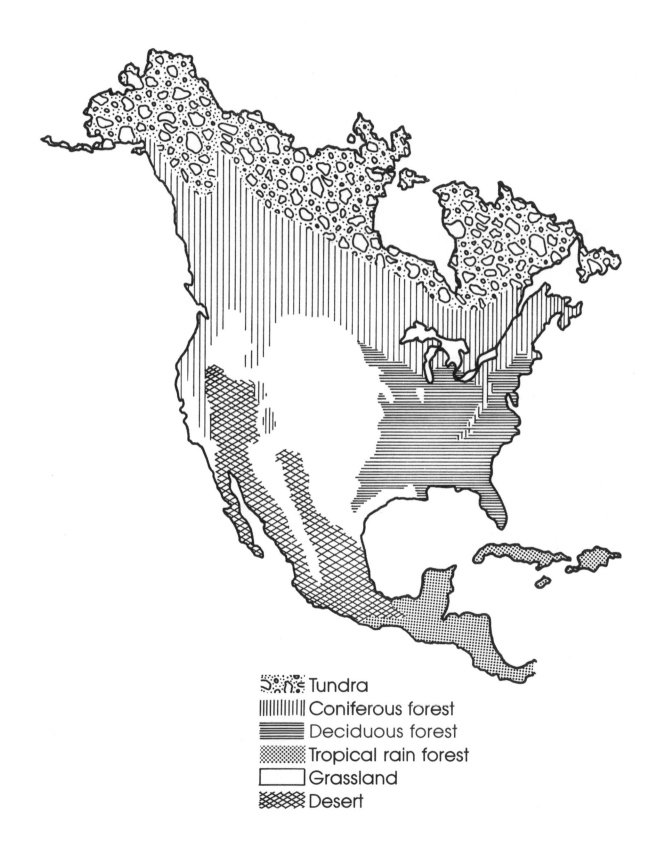

⁓∴ᴖ⁓ Tundra
|||||||||| Coniferous forest
▬▬▬ Deciduous forest
▒▒▒ Tropical rain forest
☐ Grassland
▧▧▧ Desert

97

Plant Succession

Name _____

The slow, gradual change in a community is called succession. Label the different steps of this typical succession. Number them in the correct order.

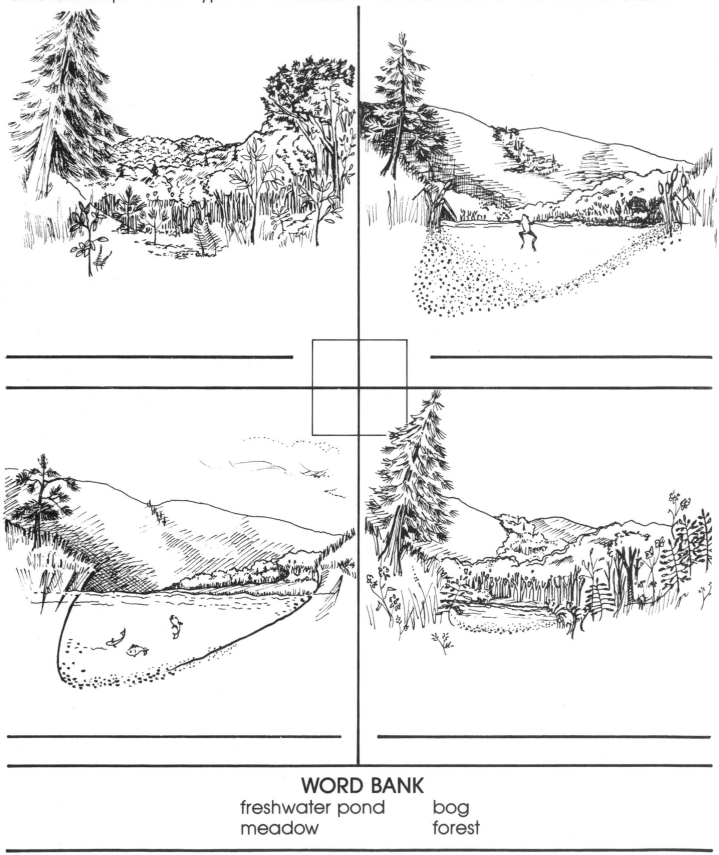

_____

_____

WORD BANK

freshwater pond	bog
meadow	forest

Vegetation Layers

Name _____

A mature forest has several layers of vegetation. Each layer supports a different kind of animal life.

Label the five layers of vegetation in the forest pictured on this page. List two animals that live in each layer.

_____

1. _____

2. _____

_____

1. _____

2. _____

_____

1. _____

2. _____

_____

1. _____

2. _____

_____

1. _____

2. _____

WORD BANK

canopy	shrub layer	forest floor
understory	herb layer	

Laboratory Equipment

Name _____

Label the pieces of laboratory equipment pictured below.

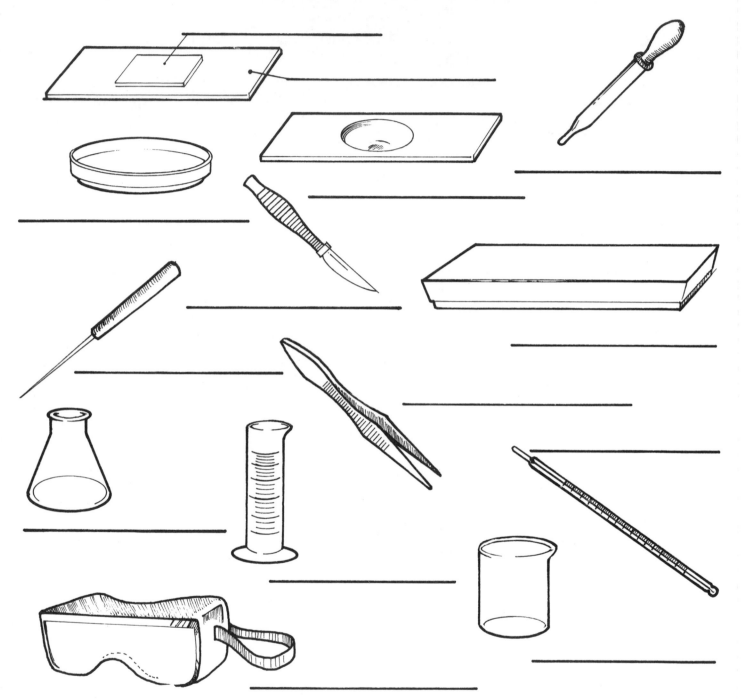

WORD BANK

dissecting pan	Petri dish	coverslip
scalpel	beaker	glass slide
forceps	thermometer	depression slide
dissecting needle	safety goggles	eyedropper
flask	graduated cylinder	

The Parts of a Microscope

Name _____

Label the parts of this compound microscope.

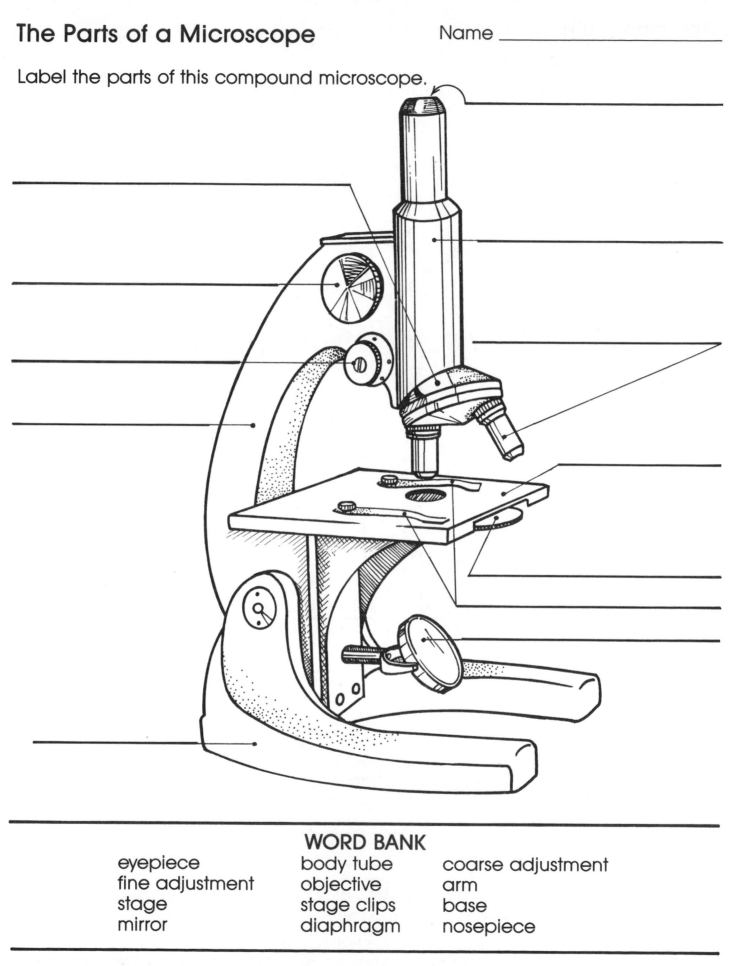

WORD BANK

eyepiece	body tube	coarse adjustment
fine adjustment	objective	arm
stage	stage clips	base
mirror	diaphragm	nosepiece

101

The Parts of a Stereomicroscope

Name _____

Label the parts of this stereomicroscope.

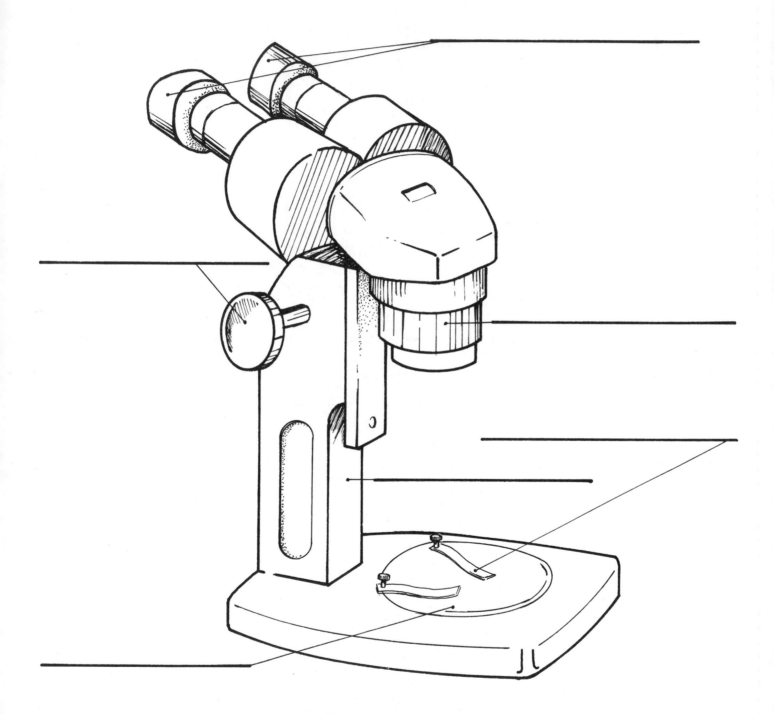

WORD BANK

single adjustment   stage   arm
eyepiece lenses   stage clips   objective lens

Answer Key

Page 1

The Five Kingdoms

Name _____

Scientists have placed all living things into five kingdoms. The organisms in each group below represent one of the five kingdoms of living things.

Label each group using the words from the WORD BANK.

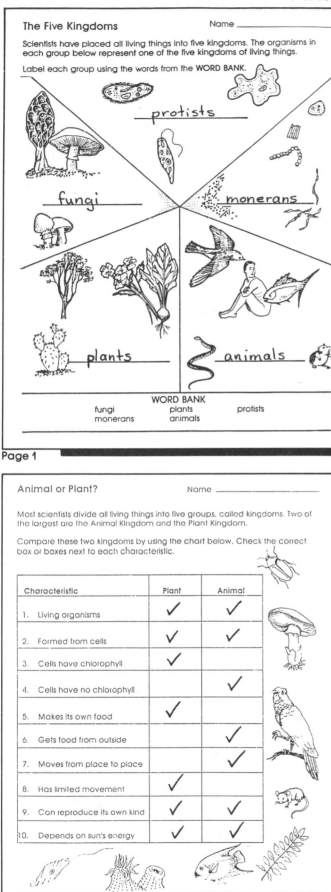

protists

fungi

monerans

plants

animals

WORD BANK

fungi
monerans

plants
animals

protists

Page 1

Page 2

Family of Living Things

Name _____

Scientists divide living things into five main groups called kingdoms. Complete the chart comparing the five kingdoms.

	Kingdoms				
	Animal	Plant	Fungus	Protist	Moneran
Does it make food? (Yes; No, Yes/No)	No	Yes	No	Yes/No	Yes/No
Does it move about? (Yes; No; Some)	Yes	No	No	Yes	Some
How many cells does it have? (One; Many)	Many	Many	Many	One or Many	One
Does the cell have a nucleus? (Yes; No)	Yes	Yes	Yes	Yes	No

Page 2

Page 3

Animal or Plant?

Name _____

Most scientists divide all living things into five groups, called kingdoms. Two of the largest are the Animal Kingdom and the Plant Kingdom.

Compare these two kingdoms by using the chart below. Check the correct box or boxes next to each characteristic.

Characteristic	Plant	Animal
1. Living organisms	✓	✓
2. Formed from cells	✓	✓
3. Cells have chlorophyll	✓	
4. Cells have no chlorophyll		✓
5. Makes its own food	✓	
6. Gets food from outside		✓
7. Moves from place to place		✓
8. Has limited movement	✓	
9. Can reproduce its own kind	✓	✓
10. Depends on sun's energy	✓	✓

Page 3

Page 4

The Plant World

Name _____

This chart shows how scientists group the many kinds of plants in the plant world.

Place a check in the column or columns that represent the plant with that characteristic.

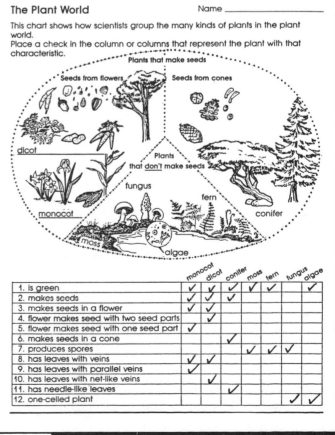

	monocot	dicot	conifer	moss	fern	fungus	algae
1. is green	✓	✓	✓	✓	✓		✓
2. makes seeds	✓	✓	✓				
3. makes seeds in a flower	✓	✓					
4. flower makes seed with two seed parts		✓					
5. flower makes seed with one seed part	✓						
6. makes seeds in a cone			✓				
7. produces spores				✓	✓	✓	
8. has leaves with veins	✓	✓					
9. has leaves with parallel veins	✓						
10. has leaves with net-like veins		✓					
11. has needle-like leaves			✓				
12. one-celled plant						✓	✓

Page 4

Answer Key

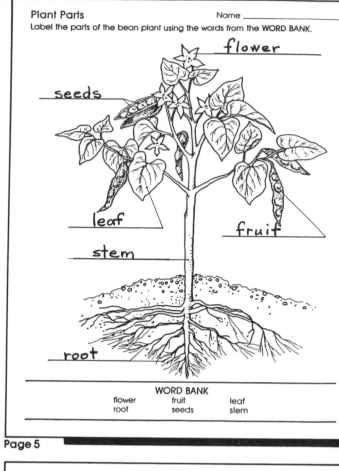
A Flowering Plant

Name _____

Label the parts of this flowering plant.

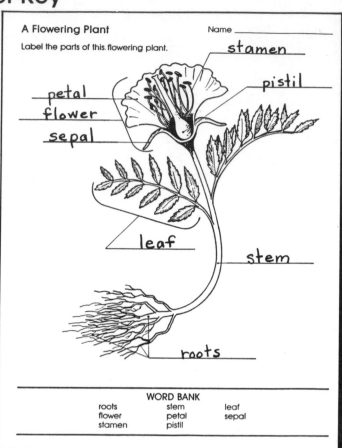

stamen
pistil
petal
flower
sepal
leaf
stem
roots

WORD BANK

roots	stem	leaf
flower	petal	sepal
stamen	pistil	

Page 6

Flower Parts

Name _____

Use the words from the WORD BANK to label the parts of the two flowers below.

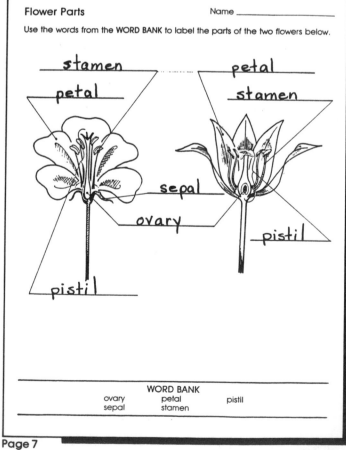

stamen
petal
petal
stamen
sepal
ovary
pistil
pistil

WORD BANK

ovary	petal	pistil
sepal	stamen	

Page 7

Seed-Producing Parts of a Flower

Name _____

Label the seed-producing parts of the flower.

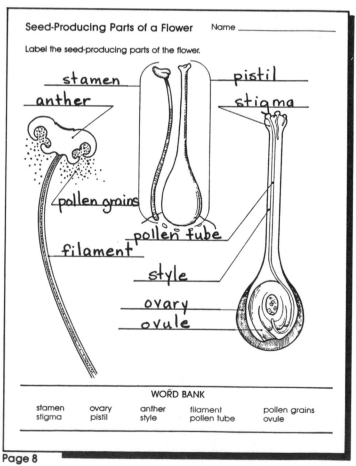

stamen
anther
pollen grains
filament
pistil
stigma
pollen tube
style
ovary
ovule

WORD BANK

stamen	ovary	anther	filament	pollen grains
stigma	pistil	style	pollen tube	ovule

Page 8

Answer Key

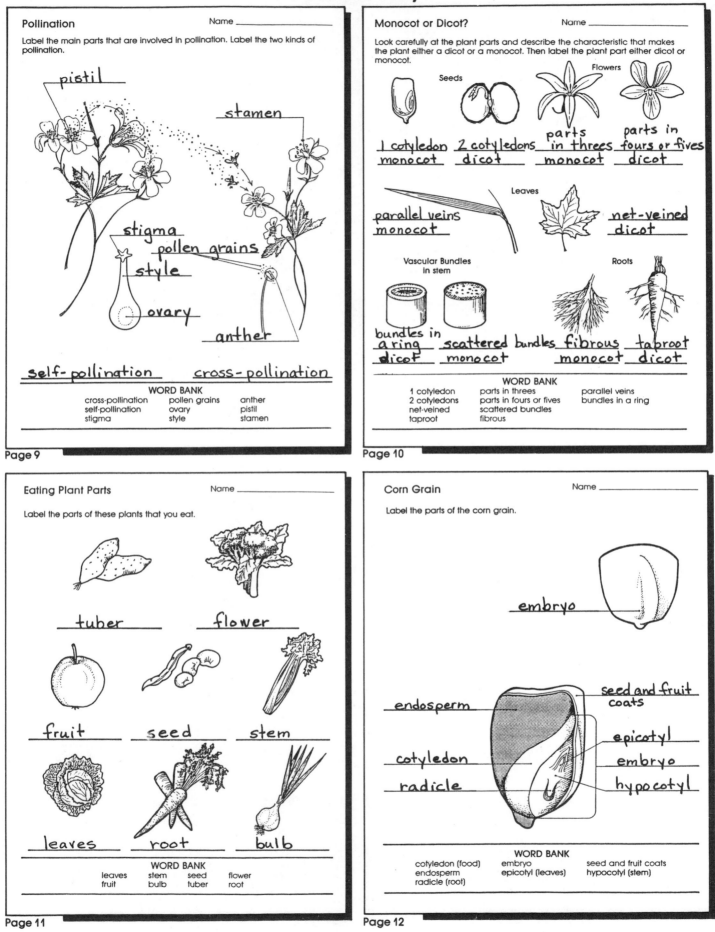

Pollination

Name _____

Label the main parts that are involved in pollination. Label the two kinds of pollination.

pistil

stamen

stigma

pollen grains

style

ovary

anther

self-pollination   cross-pollination

WORD BANK

cross-pollination	pollen grains	anther
self-pollination	ovary	pistil
stigma	style	stamen

Page 9

Monocot or Dicot?

Name _____

Look carefully at the plant parts and describe the characteristic that makes the plant either a dicot or a monocot. Then label the plant part either dicot or monocot.

Seeds

Flowers

1 cotyledon
monocot

2 cotyledons
dicot

parts in threes
monocot

parts in fours or fives
dicot

Leaves

parallel veins
monocot

net-veined
dicot

Vascular Bundles in stem

Roots

bundles in a ring
dicot

scattered bundles
monocot

fibrous
monocot

taproot
dicot

WORD BANK

1 cotyledon	parts in threes	parallel veins
2 cotyledons	parts in fours or fives	bundles in a ring
net-veined	scattered bundles	
taproot	fibrous	

Page 10

Eating Plant Parts

Name _____

Label the parts of these plants that you eat.

tuber

flower

fruit

seed

stem

leaves

root

bulb

WORD BANK

| leaves | stem | seed | flower |
| fruit | bulb | tuber | root |

Page 11

Corn Grain

Name _____

Label the parts of the corn grain.

embryo

seed and fruit coats

endosperm

epicotyl

embryo

cotyledon

radicle

hypocotyl

WORD BANK

cotyledon (food)	embryo	seed and fruit coats
endosperm	epicotyl (leaves)	hypocotyl (stem)
radicle (root)		

Page 12

© 1990 Instructional Fair, Inc.

Answer Key

Page 13

Bean Seed   Name _____

Label the parts of the bean seed.

hilum

embryo

epicotyl
hypocotyl
radicle

cotyledon

seed coat

WORD BANK

cotyledon (food)	seed coat	embryo	hilum
epicotyl (leaves)	hypocotyl (stem)	radicle (root)	

Page 13

Page 14

Growing Bean Seeds   Name _____

Label the parts of the growing bean plant.

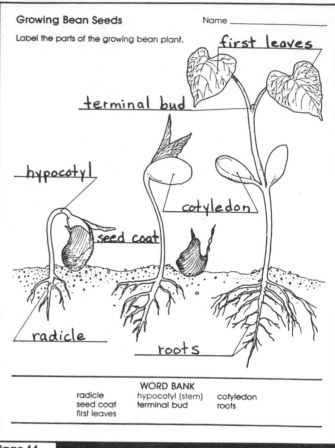

first leaves

terminal bud

hypocotyl

cotyledon

seed coat

radicle

roots

WORD BANK

radicle	hypocotyl (stem)	cotyledon
seed coat	terminal bud	roots
first leaves		

Page 14

Page 15

Tropisms   Name _____

Tropism occurs when a plant bends in response to outside stimuli such as light, gravity or water. Three common types are: **geotropism** which is caused by gravity; **phototropism** which is caused by light; and **hydrotropism** which is caused by water.

Label the type of tropism that is affecting the plant in each picture.

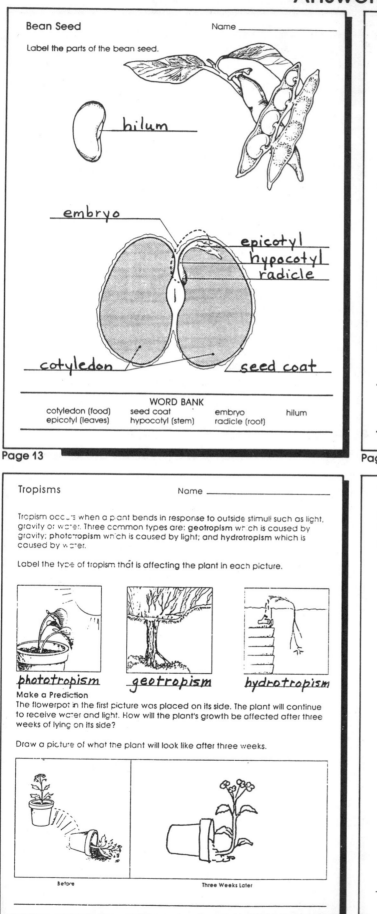

phototropism   geotropism   hydrotropism

Make a Prediction

The flowerpot in the first picture was placed on its side. The plant will continue to receive water and light. How will the plant's growth be affected after three weeks of lying on its side?

Draw a picture of what the plant will look like after three weeks.

Before   Three Weeks Later

Page 15

Page 16

Traveling Seeds   Name _____

Seeds are dispersed, or scattered, from the parent plant in many ways. The pictures below show six examples of how seeds can be dispersed.

Explain how the seeds are being dispersed in each picture.

Answers will vary.

1. Person plants seeds.
2. Squirrel planting a nut.
3. Coconut washing up on shore.
4. Bird dropping seed from mouth.
5. Burrs sticking to dog's fur.
6. Maple seed blown by wind.

Page 16

Answer Key

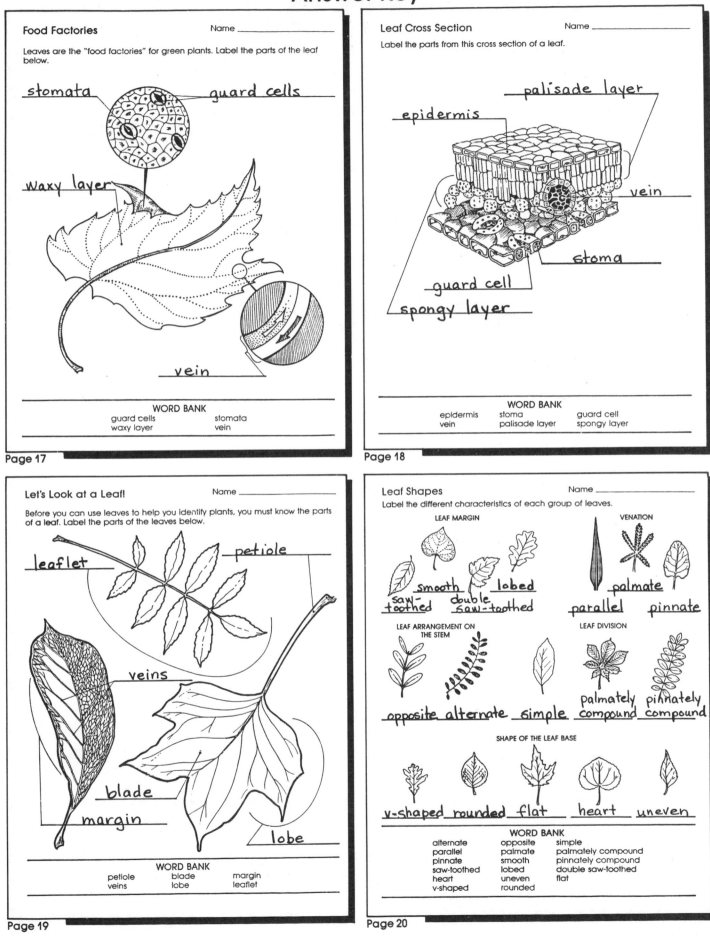

Food Factories   Name _____

Leaves are the "food factories" for green plants. Label the parts of the leaf below.

stomata   guard cells

waxy layer

vein

WORD BANK
guard cells   stomata
waxy layer   vein

Leaf Cross Section   Name _____

Label the parts from this cross section of a leaf.

palisade layer

epidermis

vein

stoma

guard cell

spongy layer

WORD BANK
epidermis   stoma   guard cell
vein   palisade layer   spongy layer

Let's Look at a Leaf!   Name _____

Before you can use leaves to help you identify plants, you must know the parts of a leaf. Label the parts of the leaves below.

leaflet   petiole

veins

blade
margin

lobe

WORD BANK
petiole   blade   margin
veins   lobe   leaflet

Leaf Shapes   Name _____

Label the different characteristics of each group of leaves.

LEAF MARGIN   **VENATION**

smooth   lobed   palmate
saw-   double   parallel   pinnate
toothed   saw-toothed

LEAF ARRANGEMENT ON   **LEAF DIVISION**
THE STEM

opposite alternate   simple   palmately   pinnately
                                 compound   compound

SHAPE OF THE LEAF BASE

v-shaped rounded flat   heart   uneven

WORD BANK
alternate   opposite   simple
parallel   palmate   palmately compound
pinnate   smooth   pinnately compound
saw-toothed lobed   double saw-toothed
heart   uneven   flat
v-shaped   rounded

Answer Key

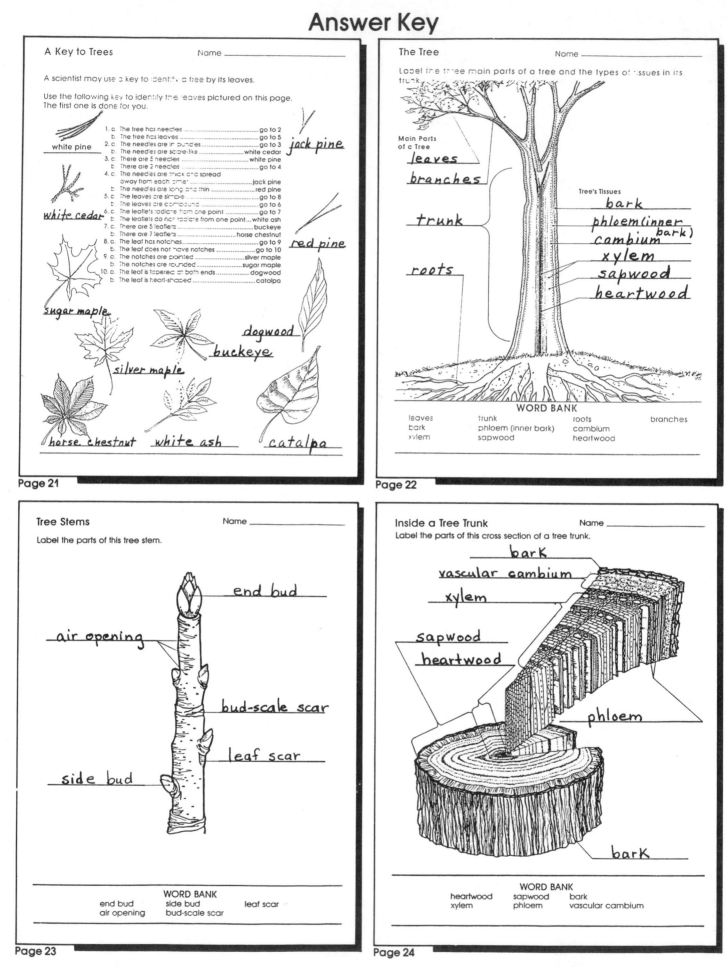

A Key to Trees

Name _____

A scientist may use a key to identify a tree by its leaves.

Use the following key to identify the leaves pictured on this page. The first one is done for you.

white pine

jack pine

1. a. The tree has needles ....go to 2
   b. The tree has leaves ....go to 5
2. a. The needles are in bundles ....go to 3
   b. The needles are scale-like ....white cedar
3. a. There are 5 needles ....white pine
   b. There are 2 needles ....go to 4
4. a. The needles are thick and spread
      away from each other ....jack pine
   b. The needles are long and thin ....red pine
5. a. The leaves are simple ....go to 8
   b. The leaves are compound ....go to 6
6. a. The leaflets radiate from one point ....go to 7
   b. The leaflets do not radiate from one point...white ash
7. a. There are 5 leaflets ....buckeye
   b. There are 7 leaflets ....horse chestnut
8. a. The leaf has notches ....go to 9
   b. The leaf does not have notches ....go to 10
9. a. The notches are pointed ....silver maple
   b. The notches are rounded ....sugar maple
10. a. The leaf is tapered at both ends ....dogwood
    b. The leaf is heart-shaped ....catalpa

white cedar

red pine

sugar maple

dogwood

buckeye

silver maple

horse chestnut

white ash

catalpa

Page 21

The Tree

Name _____

Label the three main parts of a tree and the types of tissues in its trunk.

Main Parts of a Tree

leaves

branches

trunk

roots

Tree's Tissues

bark

phloem (inner bark)

cambium

xylem

sapwood

heartwood

WORD BANK

leaves	trunk	roots	branches
bark	phloem (inner bark)	cambium	
xylem	sapwood	heartwood	

Page 22

Tree Stems

Name _____

Label the parts of this tree stem.

end bud

air opening

bud-scale scar

leaf scar

side bud

WORD BANK

end bud	side bud	leaf scar
air opening	bud-scale scar	

Page 23

Inside a Tree Trunk

Name _____

Label the parts of this cross section of a tree trunk.

bark

vascular cambium

xylem

sapwood

heartwood

phloem

bark

WORD BANK

heartwood	sapwood	bark
xylem	phloem	vascular cambium

Page 24

© 1990 Instructional Fair, Inc.

Answer Key

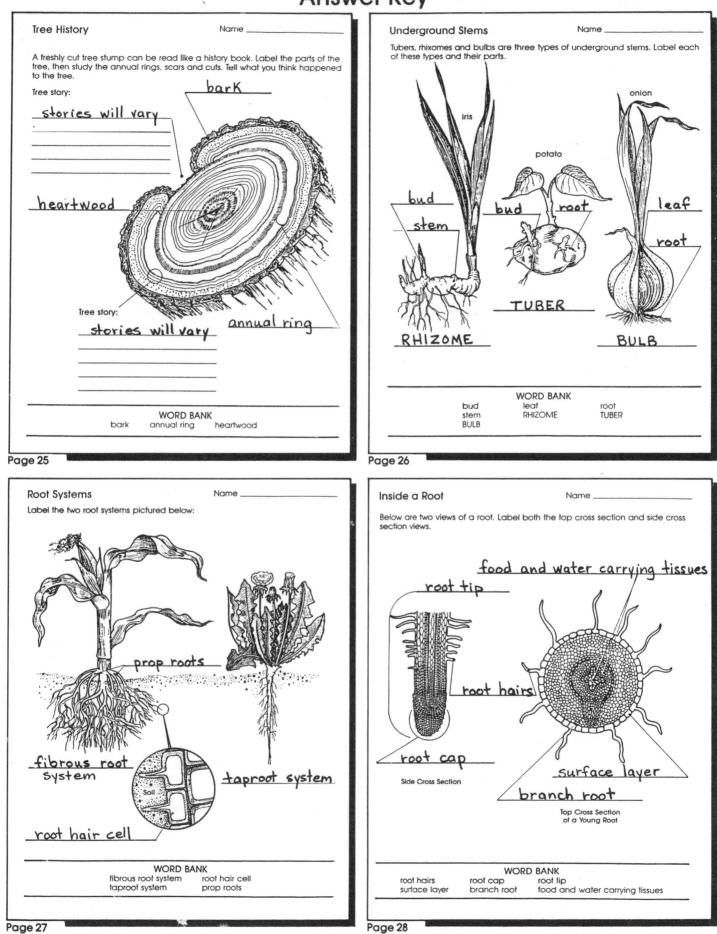

Tree History   Name _____

A freshly cut tree stump can be read like a history book. Label the parts of the tree, then study the annual rings, scars and cuts. Tell what you think happened to the tree.

Tree story:

stories will vary

bark

heartwood

Tree story:

stories will vary

annual ring

WORD BANK
bark   annual ring   heartwood

Page 25

Underground Stems   Name _____

Tubers, rhixomes and bulbs are three types of underground stems. Label each of these types and their parts.

iris

onion

potato

bud
stem

bud   root

leaf

root

RHIZOME

TUBER

BULB

WORD BANK
bud   leaf   root
stem   RHIZOME   TUBER
BULB

Page 26

Root Systems   Name _____

Label the two root systems pictured below:

prop roots

fibrous root
System

Soil

taproot system

root hair cell

WORD BANK
fibrous root system   root hair cell
taproot system   prop roots

Page 27

Inside a Root   Name _____

Below are two views of a root. Label both the top cross section and side cross section views.

food and water carrying tissues

root tip

root hairs

root cap

Side Cross Section

surface layer

branch root

Top Cross Section
of a Young Root

WORD BANK
root hairs   root cap   root tip
surface layer   branch root   food and water carrying tissues

Page 28

Life Science IF8756   109   © 1990 Instructional Fair, Inc.

Answer Key

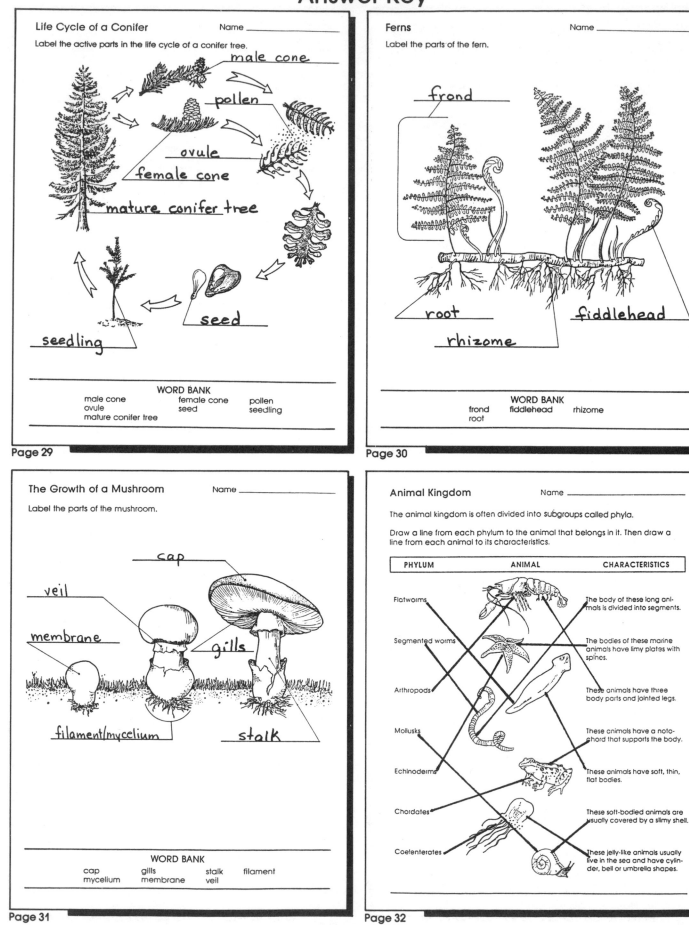

Life Cycle of a Conifer Name _____

Label the active parts in the life cycle of a conifer tree.

male cone
pollen
ovule
female cone
mature conifer tree
seed
seedling

WORD BANK

male cone	female cone	pollen
ovule	seed	seedling
mature conifer tree		

Page 29

Ferns Name _____

Label the parts of the fern.

frond
root
rhizome
fiddlehead

WORD BANK

frond	fiddlehead	rhizome
root		

Page 30

The Growth of a Mushroom Name _____

Label the parts of the mushroom.

cap
veil
membrane
gills
filament/mycelium
stalk

WORD BANK

cap	gills	stalk	filament
mycelium	membrane	veil	

Page 31

Animal Kingdom Name _____

The animal kingdom is often divided into subgroups called phyla.

Draw a line from each phylum to the animal that belongs in it. Then draw a line from each animal to its characteristics.

PHYLUM	ANIMAL	CHARACTERISTICS
Flatworms		The body of these long animals is divided into segments.
Segmented worms		The bodies of these marine animals have limy plates with spines.
Arthropods		These animals have three body parts and jointed legs.
Mollusks		These animals have a notochord that supports the body.
Echinoderms		These animals have soft, thin, flat bodies.
Chordates		These soft-bodied animals are usually covered by a slimy shell.
Coelenterates		These jelly-like animals usually live in the sea and have cylinder, bell or umbrella shapes.

Page 32

Answer Key

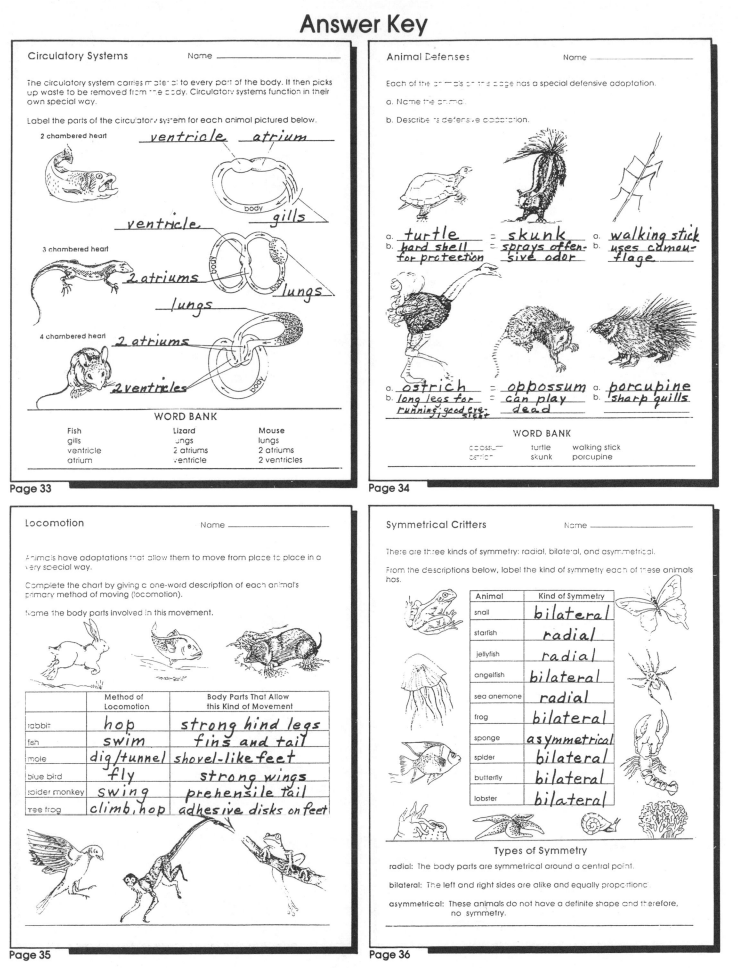

Circulatory Systems Name _____

The circulatory system carries material to every part of the body. It then picks up waste to be removed from the body. Circulatory systems function in their own special way.

Label the parts of the circulatory system for each animal pictured below.

2 chambered heart — *ventricle   atrium   body   gills*

3 chambered heart — *ventricle   2 atriums   lungs   body*

4 chambered heart — *lungs   2 atriums   2 ventricles   body*

WORD BANK

Fish	Lizard	Mouse
gills	lungs	lungs
ventricle	2 atriums	2 atriums
atrium	ventricle	2 ventricles

Page 33

Animal Defenses Name _____

Each of the animals on this page has a special defensive adaptation.

a. Name the animal.

b. Describe its defensive adaptation.

a. *turtle*   b. *hard shell for protection*

a. *skunk*   b. *sprays offensive odor*

a. *walking stick*   b. *uses camouflage*

a. *ostrich*   b. *long legs for running, good eye-sight*

a. *oppossum*   b. *can play dead*

a. *porcupine*   b. *sharp quills*

WORD BANK

opossum	turtle	walking stick
ostrich	skunk	porcupine

Page 34

Locomotion Name _____

Animals have adaptations that allow them to move from place to place in a very special way.

Complete the chart by giving a one-word description of each animal's primary method of moving (locomotion).

Name the body parts involved in this movement.

	Method of Locomotion	Body Parts That Allow this Kind of Movement
rabbit	hop	strong hind legs
fish	swim	fins and tail
mole	dig/tunnel	shovel-like feet
blue bird	fly	strong wings
spider monkey	swing	prehensile tail
tree frog	climb, hop	adhesive disks on feet

Page 35

Symmetrical Critters Name _____

There are three kinds of symmetry: radial, bilateral, and asymmetrical.

From the descriptions below, label the kind of symmetry each of these animals has.

Animal	Kind of Symmetry
snail	bilateral
starfish	radial
jellyfish	radial
angelfish	bilateral
sea anemone	radial
frog	bilateral
sponge	asymmetrical
spider	bilateral
butterfly	bilateral
lobster	bilateral

Types of Symmetry

radial: The body parts are symmetrical around a central point.

bilateral: The left and right sides are alike and equally proportioned.

asymmetrical: These animals do not have a definite shape and therefore, no symmetry.

Page 36

Answer Key

What's a Vertebrate?

Name _____

Vertebrates are grouped into five different classes. How are these classes alike, and how are they different? Complete the chart.

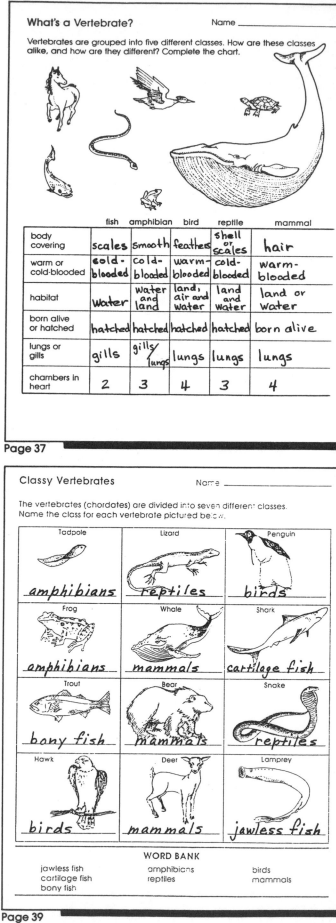

	fish	amphibian	bird	reptile	mammal
body covering	scales	smooth	feathers	shell or scales	hair
warm or cold-blooded	cold-blooded	cold-blooded	warm-blooded	cold-blooded	warm-blooded
habitat	water	water and land	land, air and water	land and water	land or water
born alive or hatched	hatched	hatched	hatched	hatched	born alive
lungs or gills	gills	gills/lungs	lungs	lungs	lungs
chambers in heart	2	3	4	3	4

Page 37

Classifying Vertebrates

Name _____

Vertebrates are sorted into five main groups called classes. Write the name of the class for each of these vertebrates.

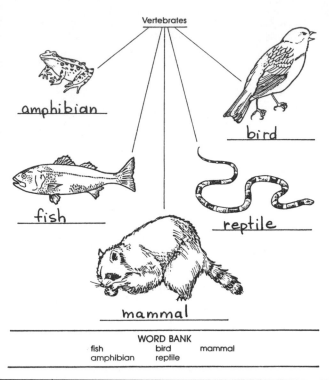

Vertebrates

amphibian

bird

fish

reptile

mammal

WORD BANK

fish   bird   mammal
amphibian   reptile

Page 38

Classy Vertebrates

Name _____

The vertebrates (chordates) are divided into seven different classes. Name the class for each vertebrate pictured below.

Tadpole	Lizard	Penguin
amphibians	reptiles	birds
Frog	**Whale**	**Shark**
amphibians	mammals	cartilage fish
Trout	**Bear**	**Snake**
bony fish	mammals	reptiles
Hawk	**Deer**	**Lamprey**
birds	mammals	jawless fish

WORD BANK

jawless fish   amphibians   birds
cartilage fish   reptiles   mammals
bony fish

Page 39

Backbones

Name _____

Animals with backbones are called vertebrates. Each of these vertebrates belongs to a different class.
Color the backbone in each of these skeletons. Write the class below each animal.

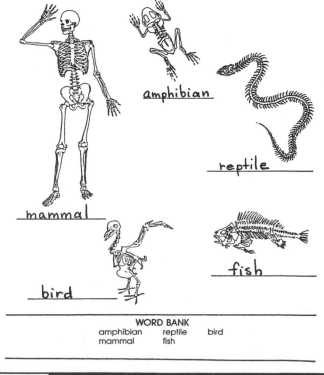

amphibian

reptile

mammal

bird

fish

WORD BANK

amphibian   reptile   bird
mammal   fish

Page 40

Answer Key

Page 41

Animals with Backbones   Name _____

Vertebrates are animals that have backbones. They are members of a group called chordates.

Write the name of the class for each set of characteristics and an example of each.

Class	Characteristics	Example
cartilage fish	-skeleton of cartilage -paired fins -cold-blooded -toothlike scales on skin	shark
jawless fish	-jawless -sucker-shaped mouth -cartilage skeleton -cold-blooded	lamprey
bony fish	-skeleton of bone -gill covers -scales -cold-blooded	trout
amphibians	-most young have gills -most adults have lungs -lay eggs in water or moist ground -cold-blooded	frog
reptiles	-dry, scaly skin -egg has tough shell -cold-blooded -well-developed lungs	lizard
birds	-feathers -wings -hollow bones -warm-blooded	hawk
mammals	-hair at same point in life -feed milk to young -well-developed brain -warm-blooded	bear

WORD BANK

mammals	amphibians	shark	hawk	reptiles
bony fish	trout	bear	birds	cartilage fish
lizard	lamprey	jawless fish	frog	

Page 41

Page 42

Vertebrates   Name _____

Vertebrates, animals with backbones, can be grouped into seven classes.

List at least four characteristics for each of the classes below.

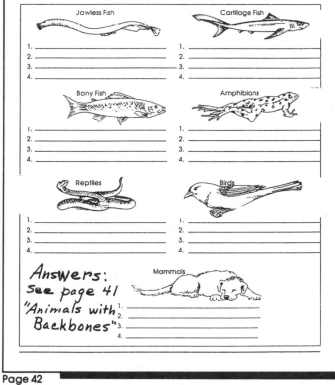

Jawless Fish
1. _____
2. _____
3. _____
4. _____

Cartilage Fish
1. _____
2. _____
3. _____
4. _____

Bony Fish
1. _____
2. _____
3. _____
4. _____

Amphibians
1. _____
2. _____
3. _____
4. _____

Reptiles
1. _____
2. _____
3. _____
4. _____

Birds
1. _____
2. _____
3. _____
4. _____

Answers: See page 41 "Animals with Backbones"

Mammals
1. _____
2. _____
3. _____
4. _____

Page 42

Page 43

Backbone or No Backbone?   Name _____

Animals with backbones are called vertebrates. Those without backbones are called invertebrates.
Label each animal as a vertebrate or invertebrate. Name each animal.

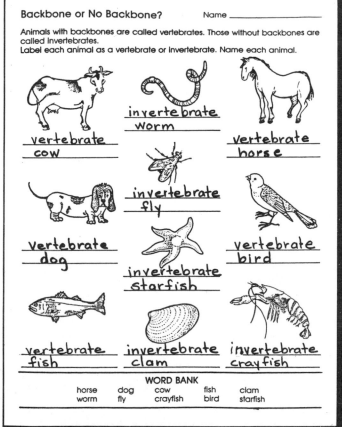

vertebrate cow

invertebrate worm

vertebrate horse

vertebrate dog

invertebrate fly

vertebrate bird

invertebrate starfish

vertebrate fish

invertebrate clam

invertebrate crayfish

WORD BANK

horse	dog	cow	fish	clam
worm	fly	crayfish	bird	starfish

Page 43

Page 44

Rippers, Nippers and Grinders   Name _____

Most mammals have two or more types of teeth: incisors for nipping food like scissors; canines for tearing food; and molars for grinding food.

Label the teeth on these animals.

Human
molars
canines
incisors

canines
incisors
Rat
molars

molars
incisors
Lion

incisors
Horse
molars

Animal	Type of Teeth	Kinds of Food Eaten
Rat	incisors, molars	grains
Lion	incisors, canines, molars	meats
Horse	incisors, molars	grasses, grains
Human	incisors, canines, molars	grains, meats, fruits, vegs. dairy prod.

WORD BANK

incisors	molars	canines
grains	grasses	meats
vegetables	dairy products	fruits

Page 44

Answer Key

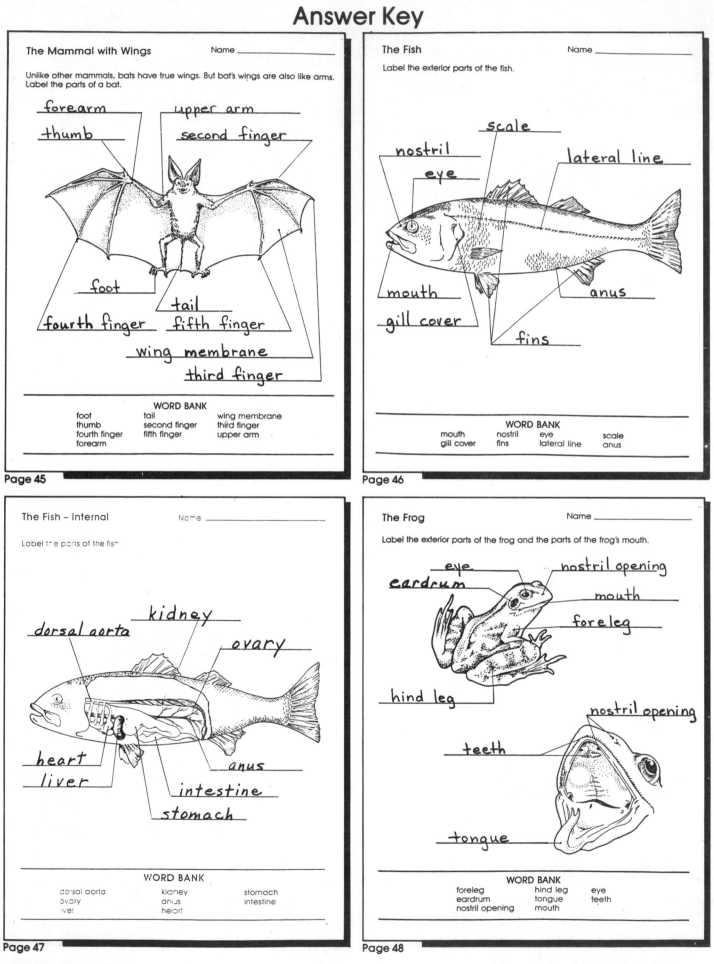

The Mammal with Wings Name _____

Unlike other mammals, bats have true wings. But bat's wings are also like arms. Label the parts of a bat.

- forearm
- upper arm
- thumb
- second finger
- foot
- tail
- fourth finger
- fifth finger
- wing membrane
- third finger

WORD BANK

foot	tail	wing membrane
thumb	second finger	third finger
fourth finger	fifth finger	upper arm
forearm		

Page 45

The Fish Name _____

Label the exterior parts of the fish.

- scale
- nostril
- lateral line
- eye
- mouth
- gill cover
- fins
- anus

WORD BANK

mouth	nostril	eye	scale
gill cover	fins	lateral line	anus

Page 46

The Fish – Internal Name _____

Label the parts of the fish

- kidney
- dorsal aorta
- ovary
- heart
- liver
- anus
- intestine
- stomach

WORD BANK

dorsal aorta	kidney	stomach
ovary	anus	intestine
liver	heart	

Page 47

The Frog Name _____

Label the exterior parts of the frog and the parts of the frog's mouth.

- eye
- nostril opening
- eardrum
- mouth
- foreleg
- hind leg
- nostril opening
- teeth
- tongue

WORD BANK

foreleg	hind leg	eye
eardrum	tongue	teeth
nostril opening	mouth	

Page 48

Answer Key

The Frog – Internal

Name _____

Label the parts of the frog.

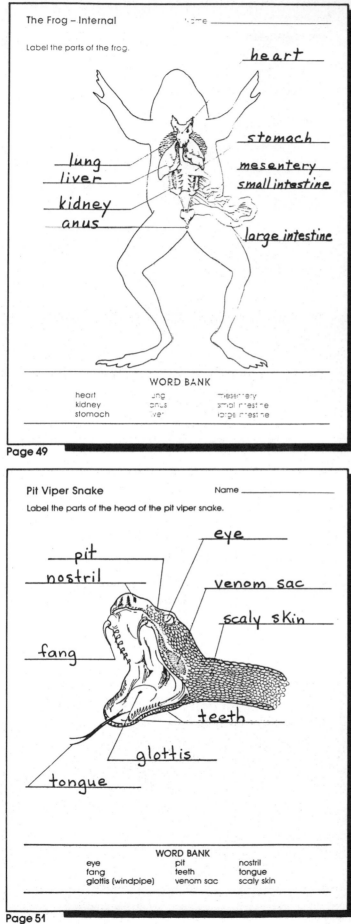

heart

stomach

mesentery

small intestine

large intestine

lung

liver

kidney

anus

WORD BANK

heart	lung	mesentery
kidney	anus	small intestine
stomach	liver	large intestine

Page 49

Life Cycle of a Frog

Name _____

Label the steps in the life cycle of the frog.

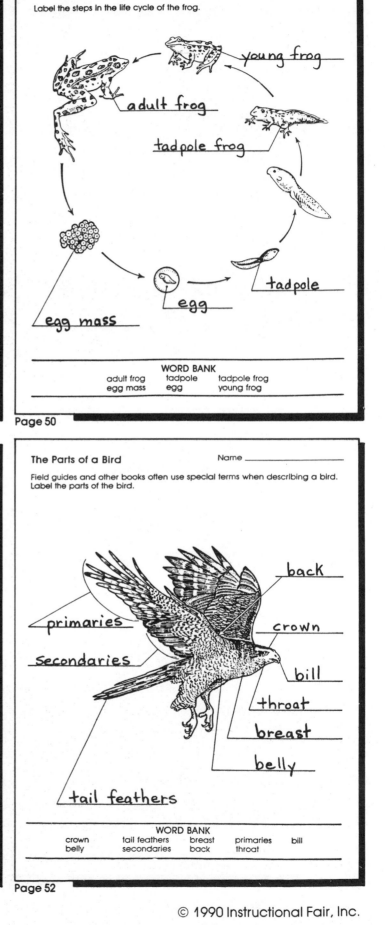

young frog

adult frog

tadpole frog

tadpole

egg

egg mass

WORD BANK

adult frog	tadpole	tadpole frog
egg mass	egg	young frog

Page 50

Pit Viper Snake

Name _____

Label the parts of the head of the pit viper snake.

eye

pit

nostril

venom sac

scaly skin

fang

teeth

glottis

tongue

WORD BANK

eye	pit	nostril
fang	teeth	tongue
glottis (windpipe)	venom sac	scaly skin

Page 51

The Parts of a Bird

Name _____

Field guides and other books often use special terms when describing a bird. Label the parts of the bird.

back

crown

bill

throat

breast

belly

primaries

secondaries

tail feathers

WORD BANK

crown	tail feathers	breast	primaries	bill
belly	secondaries	back	throat	

Page 52

Answer Key

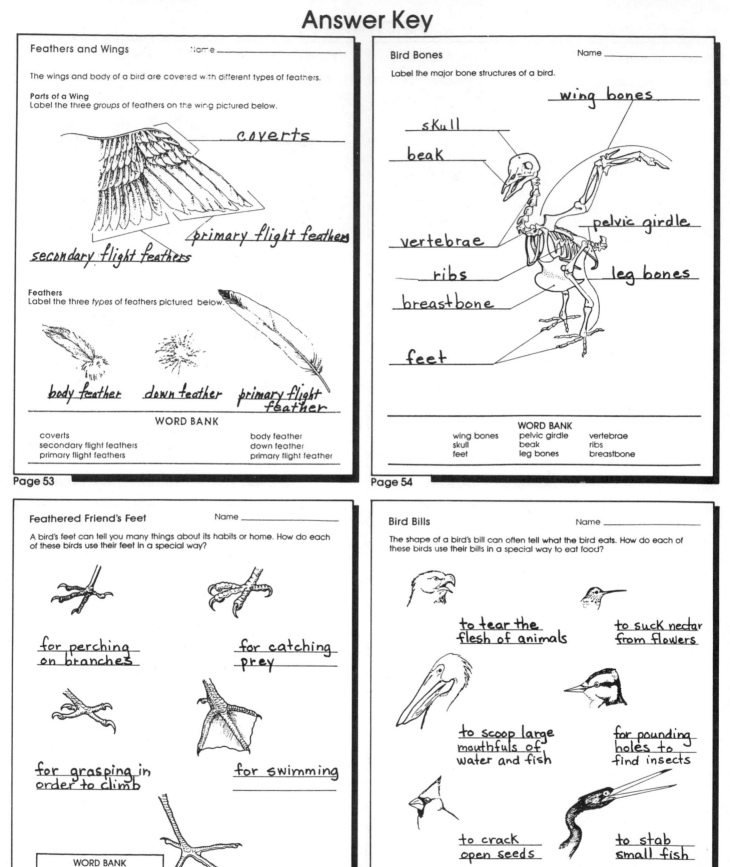

Feathers and Wings

Name _____

The wings and body of a bird are covered with different types of feathers.

Parts of a Wing
Label the three *groups* of feathers on the wing pictured below.

coverts

primary flight feathers

secondary flight feathers

Feathers
Label the three *types* of feathers pictured below.

body feather *down feather* *primary flight feather*

WORD BANK

coverts	body feather
secondary flight feathers	down feather
primary flight feathers	primary flight feather

Page 53

Bird Bones

Name _____

Label the major bone structures of a bird.

wing bones

skull

beak

vertebrae

ribs

breastbone

pelvic girdle

leg bones

feet

WORD BANK

wing bones	pelvic girdle	vertebrae
skull	beak	ribs
feet	leg bones	breastbone

Page 54

Feathered Friend's Feet

Name _____

A bird's feet can tell you many things about its habits or home. How do each of these birds use their feet in a special way?

for perching on branches

for catching prey

for grasping in order to climb

for swimming

for wading in mud

WORD BANK
for perching on branches
for wading in mud
for grasping in order to climb
for swimming
for catching prey

Page 55

Bird Bills

Name _____

The shape of a bird's bill can often tell what the bird eats. How do each of these birds use their bills in a special way to eat food?

to tear the flesh of animals

to suck nectar from flowers

to scoop large mouthfuls of water and fish

for pounding holes to find insects

to crack open seeds

to stab small fish

WORD BANK

for pounding holes to find insects	to suck nectar from flowers
to tear the flesh of animals	to stab small fish
to scoop large mouthfuls of water and fish	to crack open seeds

Page 56

Answer Key

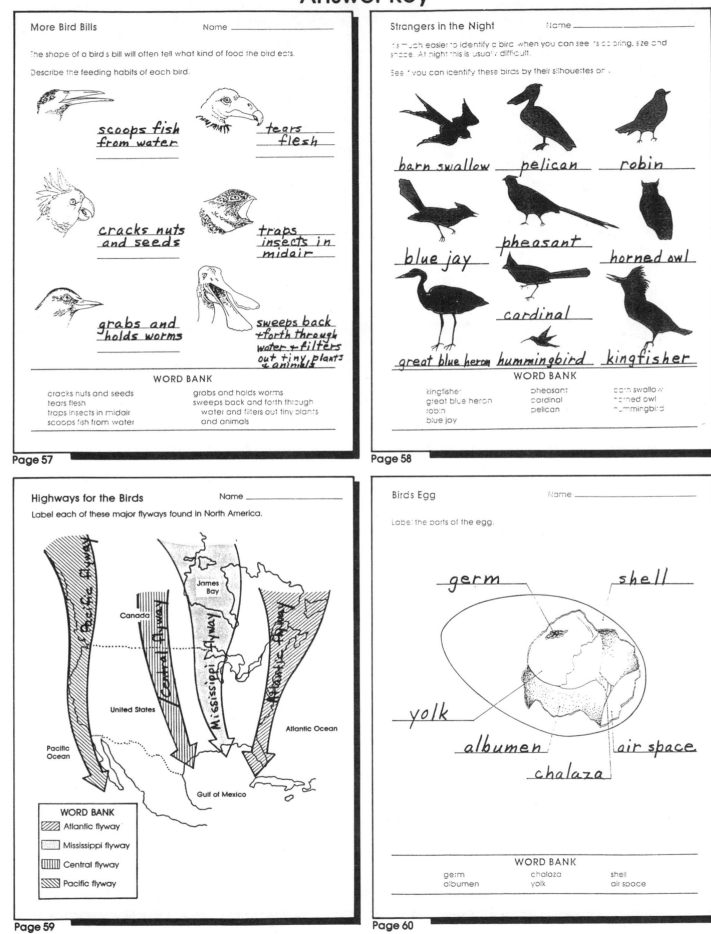

More Bird Bills   Name _____

The shape of a bird's bill will often tell what kind of food the bird eats.

Describe the feeding habits of each bird.

scoops fish from water

tears flesh

cracks nuts and seeds

traps insects in midair

grabs and holds worms

sweeps back + forth through water + filters out tiny plants & animals

WORD BANK

cracks nuts and seeds	grabs and holds worms
tears flesh	sweeps back and forth through
traps insects in midair	water and filters out tiny plants
scoops fish from water	and animals

Page 57

Strangers in the Night   Name _____

It's much easier to identify a bird when you can see its coloring, size and shape. At night this is usually difficult.

See if you can identify these birds by their silhouettes or .

barn swallow   pelican   robin

blue jay   pheasant   horned owl

cardinal

great blue heron   hummingbird   kingfisher

WORD BANK

kingfisher	pheasant	barn swallow
great blue heron	cardinal	horned owl
robin	pelican	hummingbird
blue jay		

Page 58

Highways for the Birds   Name _____

Label each of these major flyways found in North America.

Pacific Flyway

James Bay

Canada

Central Flyway

Mississippi Flyway

Atlantic Flyway

United States

Atlantic Ocean

Pacific Ocean

Gulf of Mexico

WORD BANK

- ▨ Atlantic flyway
- ▢ Mississippi flyway
- ▥ Central flyway
- ▧ Pacific flyway

Page 59

Bird's Egg   Name _____

Label the parts of the egg.

germ   shell

yolk

albumen   air space

chalaza

WORD BANK

germ	chalaza	shell
albumen	yolk	air space

Page 60

Chicken Egg

Name _____

Label the parts of this fertilized hen's egg.

air space

membrane

embryo

shell

yolk sac

WORD BANK

membrane   air space   embryo
yolk sac   shell

Classes of Arthropods

Name _____

Arthropods are animals that have jointed legs. Three-fourths of all the different animal types belong to this group.

Write the name of the class for each set of characteristics and an example of each.

Class	Characteristics	Example
diplopoda	-round -segmented body -two pairs of legs per segment	millipede
chilopoda	-flat -segmented body -one pair of legs per segment	centipede
crustacea	-hard -flexible exoskeleton -gills -two pairs of antennae -two body sections	lobster
arachnida	-two body sections -no antennae -four pairs of legs	spider
insecta	-three body sections -one pair of antennae -three pairs of legs	bee

WORD BANK

diplopoda   arachnida   centipede
chilopoda   insecta   lobster
crustacea   bee   spider
millipede

The Crayfish

Name _____

Label the parts of the crayfish.

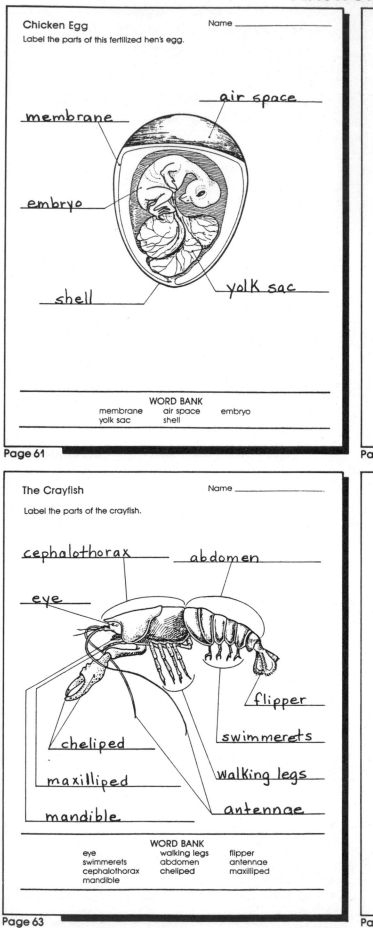

cephalothorax

abdomen

eye

flipper

swimmerets

cheliped

walking legs

maxilliped

mandible

antennae

WORD BANK

eye   walking legs   flipper
swimmerets   abdomen   antennae
cephalothorax   cheliped   maxilliped
mandible

Insect Orders

Name _____

The major groups of insects are called orders. Below are examples from several of the most common orders of insects. Label each insect and its order.

beetles
Coleoptera

butterflies
and moths
Lepidoptera

bees and wasps
Hymenoptera

grasshoppers
Orthoptera

true bugs
Hemiptera

flies
Diptera

leafhoppers
Homoptera

WORD BANK

beetles (Coleoptera)   bees and wasps (Hymenoptera)
flies (Diptera)   butterflies and moths (Lepidoptera)
grasshoppers (Orthoptera)   true bugs (Hemiptera)
leafhoppers (Homoptera)

Answer Key

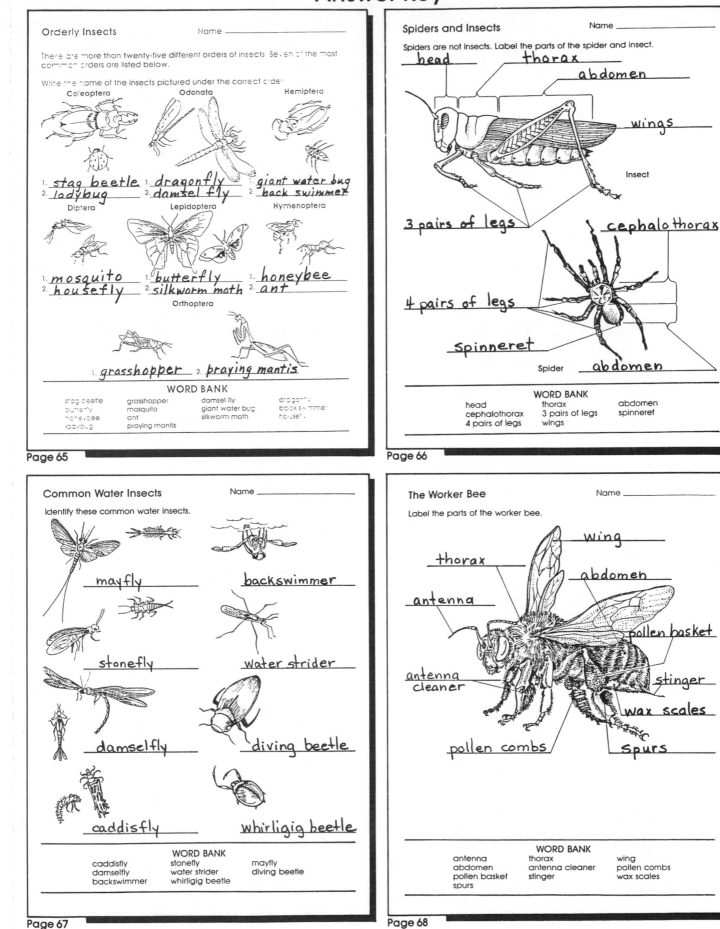

Orderly Insects

Name _____

There are more than twenty-five different orders of insects. Seven of the most common orders are listed below.

Write the name of the insects pictured under the correct order.

Coleoptera
1. stag beetle
2. ladybug

Odonata
1. dragonfly
2. damsel fly

Hemiptera
1. giant water bug
2. back swimmer

Diptera
1. mosquito
2. housefly

Lepidoptera
1. butterfly
2. silkworm moth

Hymenoptera
1. honeybee
2. ant

Orthoptera
1. grasshopper   2. praying mantis

WORD BANK
stag beetle	grasshopper	damsel fly	dragonfly
butterfly	mosquito	giant water bug	back swimmer
honeybee	ant	silkworm moth	housefly
ladybug	praying mantis		

Page 65

Spiders and Insects

Name _____

Spiders are not insects. Label the parts of the spider and insect.

head   thorax   abdomen   wings

Insect

3 pairs of legs   cephalothorax

4 pairs of legs

spinneret   abdomen

Spider

WORD BANK
head	thorax	abdomen
cephalothorax	3 pairs of legs	spinneret
4 pairs of legs	wings	

Page 66

Common Water Insects

Name _____

Identify these common water insects.

mayfly   backswimmer

stonefly   water strider

damselfly   diving beetle

caddisfly   whirligig beetle

WORD BANK
caddisfly	stonefly	mayfly
damselfly	water strider	diving beetle
backswimmer	whirligig beetle	

Page 67

The Worker Bee

Name _____

Label the parts of the worker bee.

thorax   wing   abdomen
antenna   pollen basket
antenna cleaner   stinger
wax scales
pollen combs   spurs

WORD BANK
antenna	thorax	wing
abdomen	antenna cleaner	pollen combs
pollen basket	stinger	wax scales
spurs		

Page 68

Answer Key

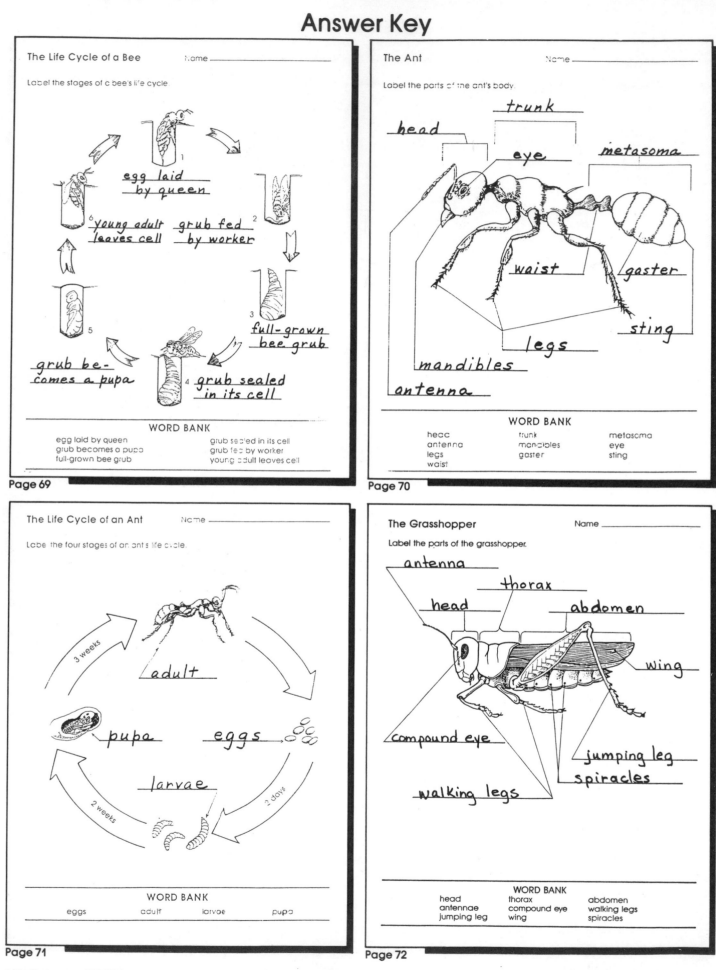

The Life Cycle of a Bee
Name _____

Label the stages of a bee's life cycle.

egg laid by queen — 1

young adult leaves cell — 6

grub fed by worker — 2

full-grown bee grub — 3

grub sealed in its cell — 4

grub becomes a pupa — 5

WORD BANK
egg laid by queen   grub sealed in its cell
grub becomes a pupa   grub fed by worker
full-grown bee grub   young adult leaves cell

The Ant
Name _____ Instructional Fair, Inc.

Label the parts of the ant's body.

head
trunk
metasoma
eye
waist   gaster
sting
legs
mandibles
antenna

WORD BANK
head   trunk   metasoma
antenna   mandibles   eye
legs   gaster   sting
waist

The Life Cycle of an Ant
Name _____

Label the four stages of an ant's life cycle.

3 weeks
adult
pupa   eggs
larvae
2 weeks   2 days

WORD BANK
eggs   adult   larvae   pupa

The Grasshopper
Name _____

Label the parts of the grasshopper.

antenna
thorax
head   abdomen
wing
compound eye
jumping leg
spiracles
walking legs

WORD BANK
head   thorax   abdomen
antennae   compound eye   walking legs
jumping leg wing   spiracles

120

© 1990 Instructional Fair, Inc.

Answer Key

The Grasshopper's Life Cycle

Name _____

The grasshopper's life cycle is an example of gradual metamorphosis. Label the steps of this cycle. You will use one word more than once.

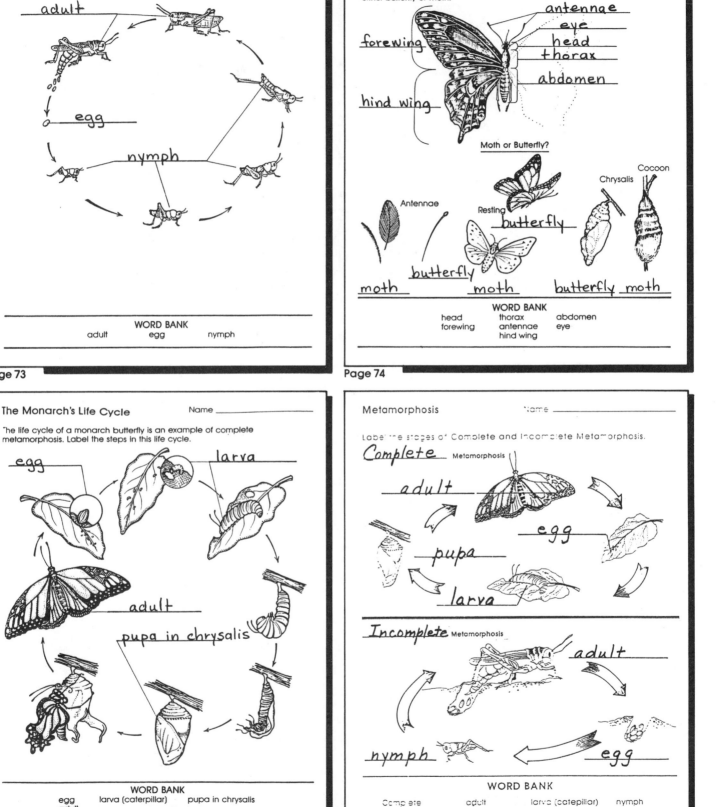

adult

egg

nymph

WORD BANK

adult   egg   nymph

Page 73

Butterflies and Moths

Name _____

Butterflies and moths belong to the order of insects called Lepidoptera. Moths and butterflies each have some special characteristics to help you tell them apart. Label the parts of the butterfly. Label the special characteristics as either butterfly or moth.

antennae
eye
head
thorax
abdomen

forewing

hind wing

Moth or Butterfly?

Antennae   Resting   butterfly   Chrysalis   Cocoon

moth   butterfly   moth   butterfly   moth

WORD BANK

head	thorax	abdomen
forewing	antennae	eye
hind wing		

Page 74

The Monarch's Life Cycle

Name _____

The life cycle of a monarch butterfly is an example of complete metamorphosis. Label the steps in this life cycle.

egg   larva

adult

pupa in chrysalis

WORD BANK

| egg | larva (caterpillar) | pupa in chrysalis |
| adult | | |

Page 75

Metamorphosis

Name _____

Label the stages of Complete and Incomplete Metamorphosis.

Complete Metamorphosis

adult

egg

pupa

larva

Incomplete Metamorphosis

adult

nymph   egg

WORD BANK

| Complete | adult | larva (caterpillar) | nymph |
| Incomplete | egg | pupa (in chrysalis) | |

Page 76

Life Science IF8756   121   © 1990 Instructional Fair, Inc.

Answer Key

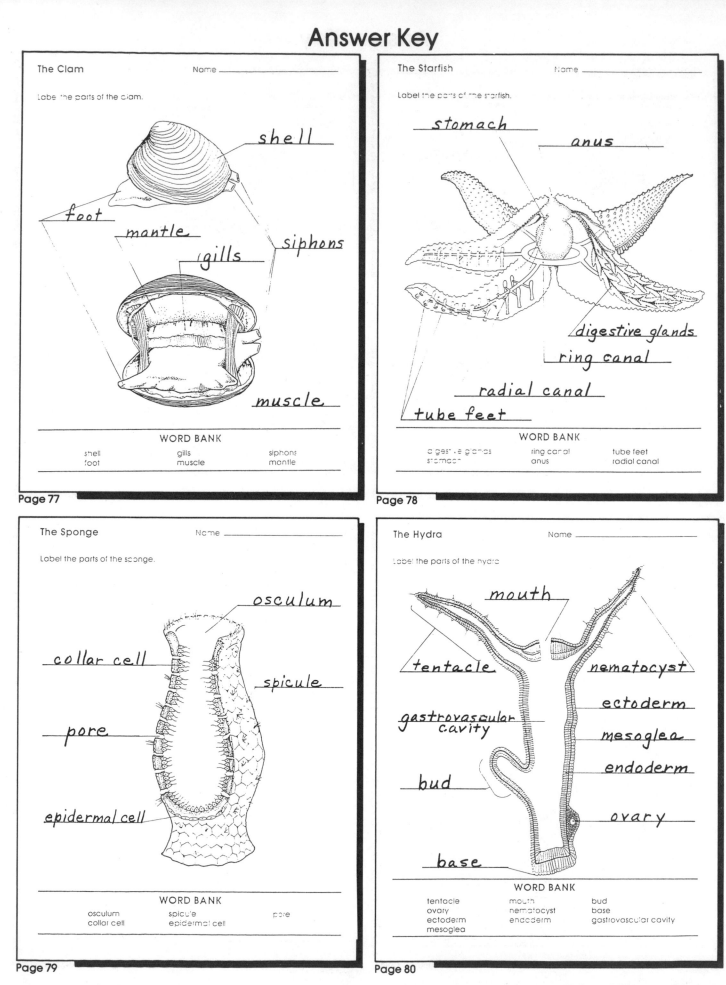

The Clam

Name _____

Lobel the parts of the clam.

shell

foot

mantle

siphons

gills

muscle

WORD BANK

shell   gills   siphons
foot   muscle   mantle

The Starfish

Name _____

Label the parts of the starfish.

stomach

anus

digestive glands

ring canal

radial canal

tube feet

WORD BANK

digestive glands   ring canal   tube feet
stomach   anus   radial canal

The Sponge

Name _____

Label the parts of the sponge.

osculum

collar cell

spicule

pore

epidermal cell

WORD BANK

osculum   spicule   pore
collar cell   epidermal cell

The Hydra

Name _____

Label the parts of the hydra.

mouth

tentacle

nematocyst

ectoderm

gastrovascular cavity

mesoglea

endoderm

bud

ovary

base

WORD BANK

tentacle   mouth   bud
ovary   nematocyst   base
ectoderm   endoderm   gastrovascular cavity
mesoglea

Answer Key

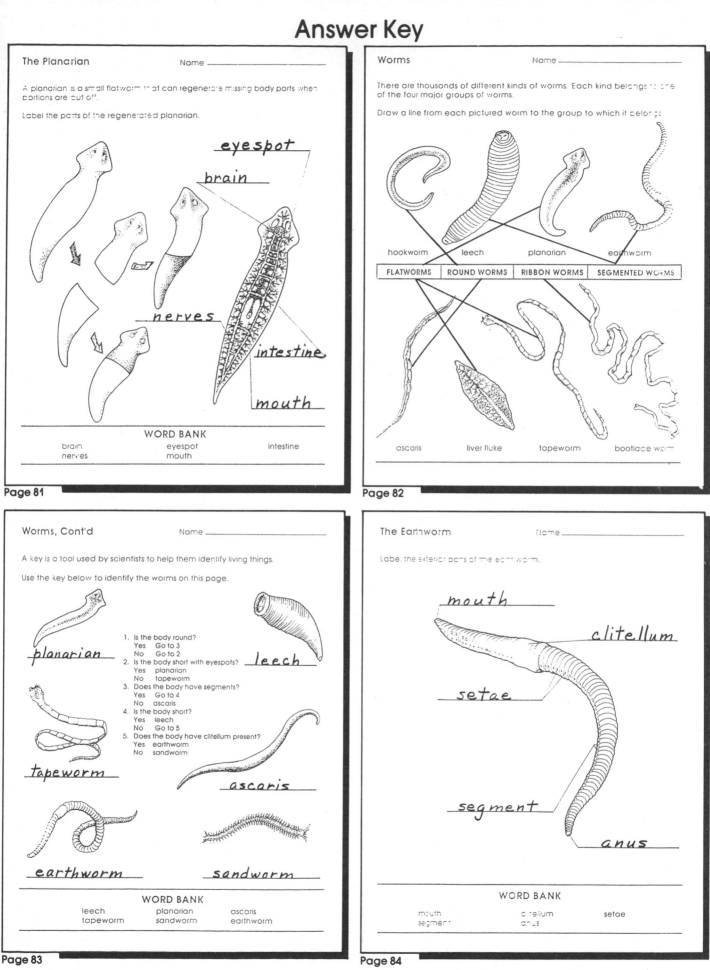

The Planarian   Name _____

A planarian is a small flatworm that can regenerate missing body parts when portions are cut off.

Label the parts of the regenerated planarian.

eyespot

brain

nerves

intestine

mouth

WORD BANK
brain	eyespot	intestine
nerves	mouth	

Page 81

Worms   Name _____

There are thousands of different kinds of worms. Each kind belongs to one of the four major groups of worms.

Draw a line from each pictured worm to the group to which it belongs.

hookworm   leech   planarian   earthworm

FLATWORMS	ROUND WORMS	RIBBON WORMS	SEGMENTED WORMS

ascaris   liver fluke   tapeworm   bootlace worm

Page 82

Worms, Cont'd   Name _____

A key is a tool used by scientists to help them identify living things.

Use the key below to identify the worms on this page.

planarian

leech

tapeworm

ascaris

earthworm

sandworm

1. Is the body round?
   Yes   Go to 3
   No   Go to 2
2. Is the body short with eyespots?
   Yes   planarian
   No   tapeworm
3. Does the body have segments?
   Yes   Go to 4
   No   ascaris
4. Is the body short?
   Yes   leech
   No   Go to 5
5. Does the body have clitellum present?
   Yes   earthworm
   No   sandworm

WORD BANK
leech	planarian	ascaris
tapeworm	sandworm	earthworm

Page 83

The Earthworm   Name _____

Label the exterior parts of the earthworm.

mouth

clitellum

setae

segment

anus

WORD BANK
mouth	clitellum	setae
segment	anus	

Page 84

Life Science IF8756   123   © 1990 Instructional Fair, Inc.

Answer Key

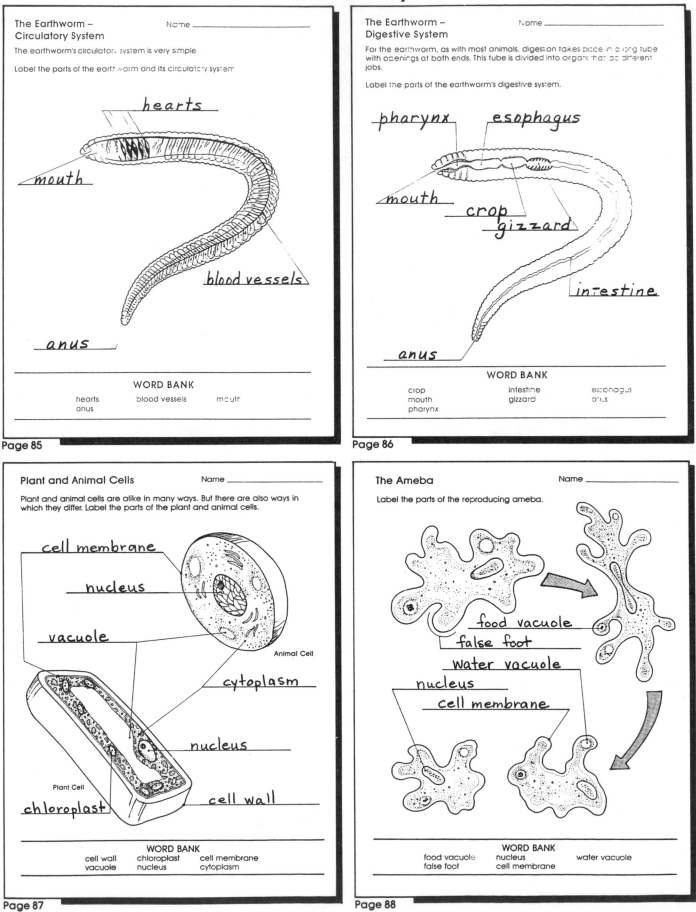

The Earthworm – Circulatory System

Name _____

The earthworm's circulatory system is very simple

Label the parts of the earthworm and its circulatory system.

hearts

mouth

blood vessels

anus

WORD BANK

hearts   blood vessels   mouth
anus

Page 85

The Earthworm – Digestive System

Name _____

For the earthworm, as with most animals, digestion takes place in a long tube with openings at both ends. This tube is divided into organs that do different jobs.

Label the parts of the earthworm's digestive system.

pharynx   esophagus

mouth

crop

gizzard

intestine

anus

WORD BANK

crop   intestine   esophagus
mouth   gizzard   anus
pharynx

Page 86

Plant and Animal Cells

Name _____

Plant and animal cells are alike in many ways. But there are also ways in which they differ. Label the parts of the plant and animal cells.

cell membrane

nucleus

vacuole

Animal Cell

cytoplasm

nucleus

Plant Cell

chloroplast

cell wall

WORD BANK

cell wall   chloroplast   cell membrane
vacuole   nucleus   cytoplasm

Page 87

The Ameba

Name _____

Label the parts of the reproducing ameba.

food vacuole

false foot

water vacuole

nucleus

cell membrane

WORD BANK

food vacuole   nucleus   water vacuole
false foot   cell membrane

Page 88

Answer Key

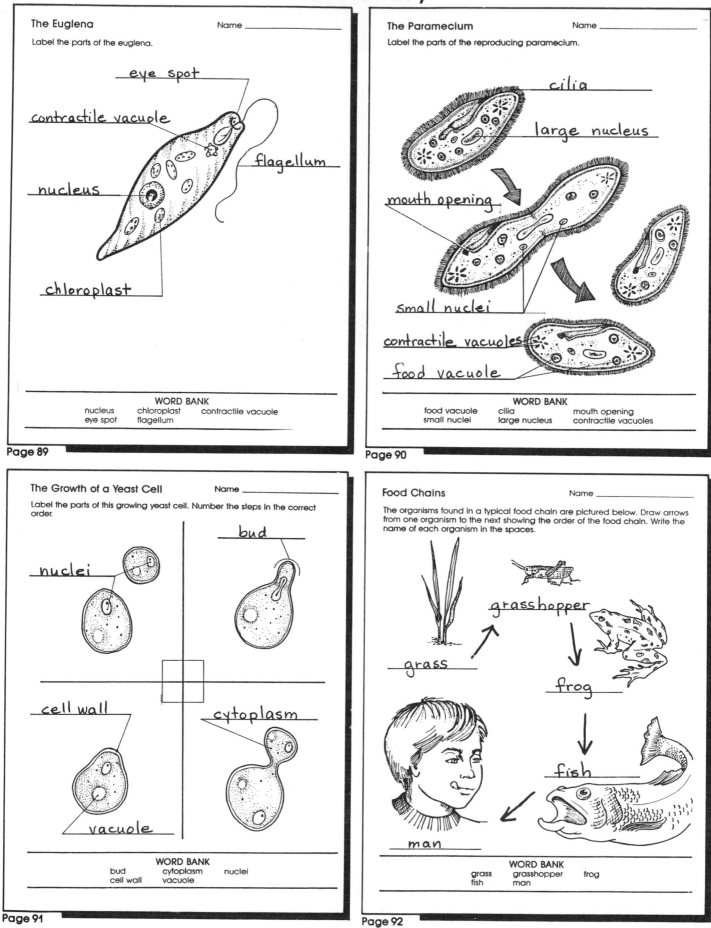

The Euglena   Name _____

Label the parts of the euglena.

- eye spot
- contractile vacuole
- flagellum
- nucleus
- chloroplast

WORD BANK

| nucleus | chloroplast | contractile vacuole |
| eye spot | flagellum | |

Page 89

The Paramecium   Name _____

Label the parts of the reproducing paramecium.

- cilia
- large nucleus
- mouth opening
- small nuclei
- contractile vacuoles
- food vacuole

WORD BANK

| food vacuole | cilia | mouth opening |
| small nuclei | large nucleus | contractile vacuoles |

Page 90

The Growth of a Yeast Cell   Name _____

Label the parts of this growing yeast cell. Number the steps in the correct order.

- nuclei
- bud
- cell wall
- cytoplasm
- vacuole

WORD BANK

| bud | cytoplasm | nuclei |
| cell wall | vacuole | |

Page 91

Food Chains   Name _____

The organisms found in a typical food chain are pictured below. Draw arrows from one organism to the next showing the order of the food chain. Write the name of each organism in the spaces.

- grasshopper
- grass
- frog
- fish
- man

WORD BANK

| grass | grasshopper | frog |
| fish | man | |

Page 92

Answer Key

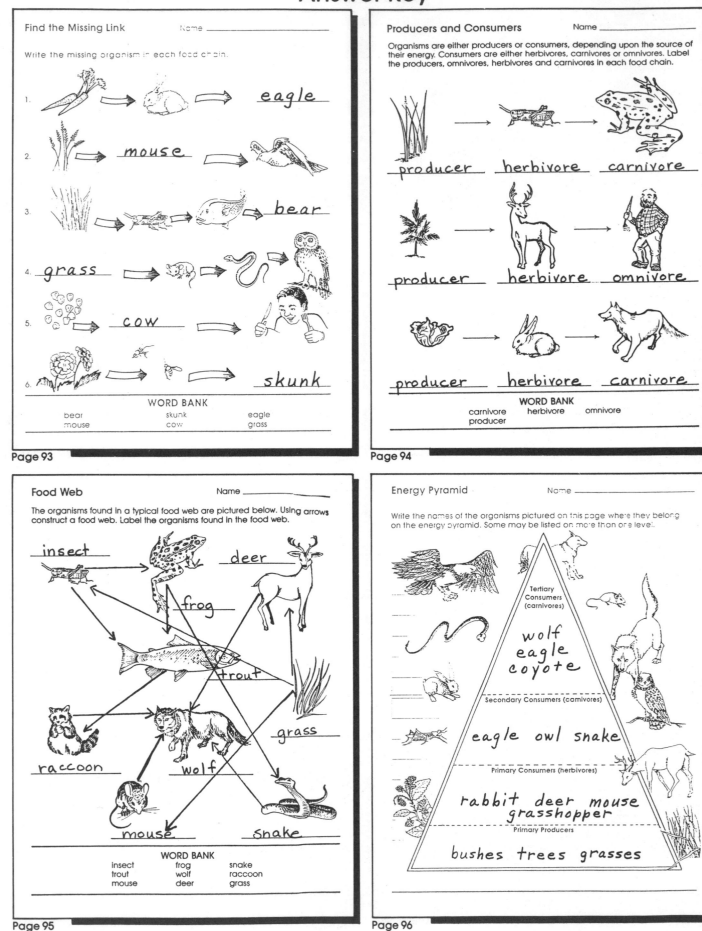

Find the Missing Link

Write the missing organism in each food chain.

1. carrot → rabbit → *eagle*
2. wheat → *mouse* → hawk
3. cattails → grasshopper → fish → *bear*
4. *grass* → mouse → snake → owl
5. *cow* → person
6. flower → bee → *skunk*

WORD BANK

bear	skunk	eagle
mouse	cow	grass

Page 93

Producers and Consumers

Organisms are either producers or consumers, depending upon the source of their energy. Consumers are either herbivores, carnivores or omnivores. Label the producers, omnivores, herbivores and carnivores in each food chain.

producer — *herbivore* — *carnivore*

producer — *herbivore* — *omnivore*

producer — *herbivore* — *carnivore*

WORD BANK

carnivore	herbivore	omnivore
producer		

Page 94

Food Web

The organisms found in a typical food web are pictured below. Using arrows construct a food web. Label the organisms found in the food web.

insect   *frog*   *deer*

trout

raccoon   *wolf*   *grass*

mouse   *snake*

WORD BANK

insect	frog	snake
trout	wolf	raccoon
mouse	deer	grass

Page 95

Energy Pyramid

Write the names of the organisms pictured on this page where they belong on the energy pyramid. Some may be listed on more than one level.

Tertiary Consumers (carnivores)

wolf eagle coyote

Secondary Consumers (carnivores)

eagle owl snake

Primary Consumers (herbivores)

rabbit deer mouse grasshopper

Primary Producers

bushes trees grasses

Page 96

Life Science IF8756   126   © 1990 Instructional Fair, Inc.

Answer Key

Biomes of North America

Name _____

Color the map and key to identify the major biomes of North America.

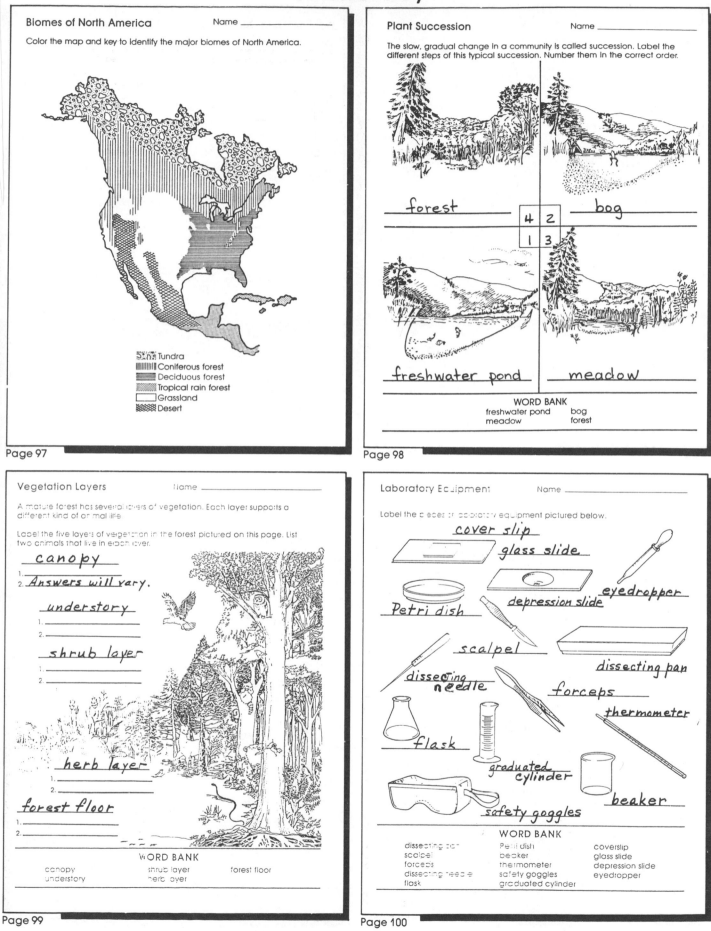

Tundra
Coniferous forest
Deciduous forest
Tropical rain forest
Grassland
Desert

Plant Succession

Name _____

The slow, gradual change in a community is called succession. Label the different steps of this typical succession. Number them in the correct order.

forest   bog

4	2
1	3

freshwater pond   meadow

WORD BANK
freshwater pond   bog
meadow   forest

Vegetation Layers

Name _____

A mature forest has several layers of vegetation. Each layer supports a different kind of animal life.

Label the five layers of vegetation in the forest pictured on this page. List two animals that live in each layer.

canopy
1.
2. Answers will vary.

understory
1.
2.

shrub layer
1.
2.

herb layer
1.
2.

forest floor
1.
2.

WORD BANK
canopy   shrub layer   forest floor
understory   herb layer

Laboratory Equipment

Name _____

Label the pieces of laboratory equipment pictured below.

cover slip
glass slide
eyedropper
Petri dish
depression slide
scalpel
dissecting pan
dissecting needle
forceps
thermometer
flask
graduated cylinder
safety goggles
beaker

WORD BANK
dissecting pan   Petri dish   coverslip
scalpel   beaker   glass slide
forceps   thermometer   depression slide
dissecting needle   safety goggles   eyedropper
flask   graduated cylinder

Answer Key

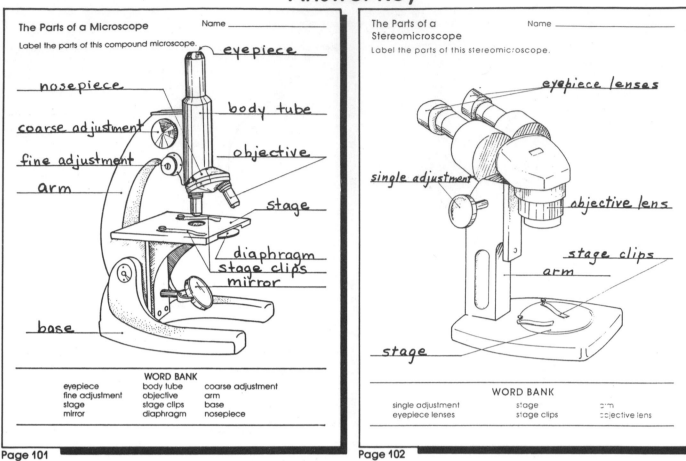

The Parts of a Microscope   Name _____

Label the parts of this compound microscope.

- eyepiece
- nosepiece
- body tube
- coarse adjustment
- objective
- fine adjustment
- arm
- stage
- diaphragm
- stage clips
- mirror
- base

WORD BANK

eyepiece	body tube	coarse adjustment
fine adjustment	objective	arm
stage	stage clips	base
mirror	diaphragm	nosepiece

Page 101

The Parts of a Stereomicroscope   Name _____

Label the parts of this stereomicroscope.

- eyepiece lenses
- single adjustment
- objective lens
- stage clips
- arm
- stage

WORD BANK

single adjustment	stage	arm
eyepiece lenses	stage clips	objective lens

Page 102

About the book . . .

    Life Science is a collection of true-to-life drawings showing a variety of systems, cycles, orders, etc. in the five kingdoms of living things designed for use as labeling activities. These activities will serve as excellent supplements for any comprehensive study of science or biology.

About the author . . .

    Daryl Vriesenga holds a Master's Degree from Michigan State University in Science Education. He has taught at the elementary level for over seventeen years. He is the author of several science books for the elementary classroom.

Author: Daryl Vriesenga
Editor: Lee Quackenbush/Lisa Hancock
Editorial Assistant: Carolyn Carbery
Artist: Ann Stein
Project Director: Sharon Kirkwood
Production: Pat Geasler
Cover Photo: Frank Pieroni
Art Constultant: Jan Vonk